The Australian Women's Weekly — Home Library

CHILDREN'S BIRTHDAY CAKE BOOK

Food Editor ELLEN SINCLAIR says: "Here's the book you've been asking for — more than a hundred exciting party cakes to choose from for the important birthday!" They're easy to make and the whole family will enjoy looking at the colourful pictures while the children choose their special birthday cake

Editor-in-Chief
Trevor Kennedy

Production Editor
Kerrie Lee

Art Director
Rowena Sheppard

Photographer
Russell Brooks

Our cover: Train, see page 124.

Pictured opposite: Puss In Boots, see page 18.

Type set by Photoset Computer Service Pty Ltd, Sydney, Australia.

Printed by Dai Nippon Printing Co Ltd, Tokyo, Japan.

Published by Australian Consolidated Press Ltd, 168 Castlereagh Street, Sydney, Australia.
*Recommended and maximum price only.

BEFORE YOU START TO

Here's all the information you need to help make the important birthday cake a great success! Recipes for popular cake coverings — Vienna Cream and Fluffy Frosting — are given, as well as full instructions on how to colour coconut, make decorations, prepare cake boards for use and estimate the cooking times

CAKES TO USE

We have specified butter cake packet mixes in each recipe because they're easy to make and give a firm foundation for decorations on the birthday cake. Plain, chocolate or any other flavour can be used. If you prefer to make your own cake, here is a recipe for a good home-made butter cake, which is equivalent in quantity to a packet cake mix.

BUTTER CAKE
125g (4oz) butter
½ teaspoon vanilla
½ cup castor sugar
2 eggs
1½ cups self-raising flour
⅓ cup milk

Have butter at room temperature, beat butter with vanilla until light and creamy, add sugar, beat until light and fluffy; add eggs one at a time, beating well after each addition. Stir in half the sifted flour with half the milk, stir until combined. Add remaining milk and flour, stir in lightly, then beat lightly until mixture is smooth. Spread into greased tin, bake as directed in individual recipes. Cooking times are the same as for packet butter cake mix.

PREPARATION OF CAKES

Cakes are best made the day before the party as they are much easier to cut and to ice and decorate when one day old; if too fresh, crumbs from the cake will stick to the icing. In fact, cakes can be made up to a month in advance and frozen in airtight bags; allow to thaw in refrigerator section for 12 hours before using.

Grease cake tins lightly but evenly; use a pastry brush and melted butter for best results. When cakes are cooked, remove from oven, stand for three minutes, shake the tin gently to make sure cake is free from base and sides, then turn on to wire rack to cool. Most cakes in this book use the smooth base for the top of the finished cake, so leave cakes to cool upside down to avoid getting marks from wire racks on the base. In the case of cakes which require the rounded tops to decorate, cool right side up. Individual recipes indicate where this is necessary.

Following is a guide to sizes of tins and oven temperatures using one packet of cake mix or one quantity of basic Butter Cake. Some recipes use only part of a cake mix; in these instances, cooking times will of course vary as indicated in individual recipes. Bake all cakes so that the top will be as close as possible to the centre of the oven. Ovens vary so times given should be taken only as a general guide. When cooked, cakes should be starting just to shrink from sides of tin and a skewer, when inserted in centre, should come out completely free of cake mixture.

Cakes given below are all cooked in a moderate oven — that is, 190 to 200 degrees C (375 to 400 degrees F) in electric or 180 degrees C (350 degrees F) in a gas oven.

COOKING TIMES

28cm × 18cm (11in × 7in) lamington tin	30 minutes
20cm (8in) ring tin	35 minutes
30cm × 25cm (12in × 10in) swiss roll tin	20 minutes
2 × 25cm × 8cm (10in × 3in) bar tins	30 minutes
20cm × 10cm (8in × 4in) loaf tin	50 minutes
23cm × 12cm (9in × 5in) loaf tin	50 minutes
25cm × 15cm (10in × 6in) loaf tin	45 minutes
Deep 18cm (7in) round cake tin	1 hour 10 minutes
Deep 20cm (8in) round cake tin	50 minutes
Deep 23cm (9in) round cake tin	45 minutes
Deep 15cm (6in) square cake tin	1 hour 10 minutes
Deep 20cm (8in) square cake tin	55 minutes

VIENNA CREAM
125g (4oz) butter
1½ cups icing sugar
2 tablespoons milk

Have butter and milk at room temperature, place butter in small bowl of electric mixer, beat until butter is as white as possible, gradually add about half the sifted icing sugar, beating constantly, add milk gradually, then gradually beat in the remaining icing sugar; mixture should be smooth and easy to spread with a spatula.

CHOCOLATE VIENNA CREAM
Make up the basic recipe as above and add 2 tablespoons sifted cocoa to the icing sugar.

COLOURED VIENNA CREAM
A large variety of food colourings is available at supermarkets and health food stores, for about 30 cents a small bottle. As only a very small amount is used each time, the bottle will last a long time. Each recipe in this book indicates the colour we used but of course you can make your own choice of colourings.

Start to tint Vienna Cream (or any icing) by dipping a skewer into the bottle of colouring, shaking off excess, then dipping the skewer into icing; beat well with a wooden spoon. Every bottle of colouring will vary in strength; by adding it with a skewer you avoid over-colouring. Make sure the colouring is beaten evenly through the Vienna Cream.

ICING SUGAR
Pure icing sugar or icing sugar mixture can be used in Vienna Cream. Sift icing sugar through a fine sieve for best results.

Make Vienna Cream on the day it is to be used; keep covered during use as a crust will develop if it is left uncovered. Do not refrigerate cream as this will cause the butter to harden and it may separate.

For best results Vienna Cream should be applied to a cake on the day it is to be served. You can apply it the day before serving but, if you do, the cream will become slightly darker and crusty in appearance.

When applying Vienna Cream, make sure it covers the cake around the base near the board to form a seal and help keep the cake fresh. Use a small spatula when applying Vienna Cream as this will give a smooth surface to the cake.

Cream will spread easily but, if you want a particularly smooth surface, dip the spatula in hot water, dry quickly, use hot to spread the cream.

MAKE THE CAKE...

FLUFFY FROSTING
TWO EGG WHITE QUANTITY
1 cup sugar
⅓ cup water
2 egg whites
THREE EGG WHITE QUANTITY
1¼ cups sugar
½ cup water
3 egg whites

Combine sugar and water in small saucepan, stir over medium heat until sugar is dissolved, do not boil; brush any sugar grains down from side of saucepan with brush dipped in water. Increase heat, boil rapidly, uncovered, for 3 to 5 minutes; do not stir after syrup boils. If a sweets thermometer is available, syrup should reach 115 degrees C (240 degrees F), otherwise you can test by dropping 1 teaspoon of syrup into cold water; it should form a ball of soft sticky toffee when rolled between fingers. If testing syrup in water, remove pan from heat when syrup falls from spoon in a heavy drop, allow bubbles to subside, then test in cold water. The syrup should not change colour; if it does, it has been

cooked for too long and you will have to throw out that batch and start the process again.

While syrup is boiling, beat egg whites in small bowl of electric mixer until stiff, keep beating (or whites will deflate) while syrup is reaching the correct temperature. When syrup is ready, allow bubbles to subside, pour in a very thin stream on to the egg whites while they are beating on medium speed. Picture shows the thin stream of syrup being added; if it is added too quickly, frosting will not thicken. Continue beating and adding syrup until all syrup is used. Continue to beat until frosting will stand in stiff peaks (frosting should be only warm at this stage). Tint, if desired, by beating colour through in mixer or with wooden spoon, spread over cake as directed in individual recipes. Frosting also can be flavoured with ½ teaspoon of any essence.

For best results, frosting should be applied to a cake on the day it is to be served when frosting is beautifully soft, with a marshmallow consistency.

However, the cake can be frosted the day before and all that will happen is that frosting will become slightly crisp because it has dried out a little and will lose its glossy appearance. When applying frosting, make sure it covers the cake around the base near the board; this will form a seal and help keep the cake fresh.

Pour a thin stream of syrup on to the egg whites while beating on medium speed of electric mixer.

HOW TO COLOUR COCONUT
Place required amount of coconut in a bowl, add two or three drops of food colouring; wet hands with cold water, shake off excess water, rub colouring through coconut. Add more colouring as required. Both shredded and desiccated coconut can be coloured in this way.

Food colouring will stain hands. To prevent this, wear clean, fine rubber gloves, such as surgical gloves (obtainable from chemist shops for under $1); wet the gloves with cold water, as mentioned above.

Any leftover coconut can be kept in a screw-top jar in the refrigerator until it is required.

DECORATIONS ON THE CAKES
All decorations used on cakes in this book were bought from supermarkets, chain stores, toy sections of department stores or toy shops. Ballerinas (page 96) are available from cake sections of department stores and from cake shops.
LICORICE ALLSORTS
The black licorice pieces can be used for doors, windows, shutters and so on. Coloured fondant in the centres can be stuck on to toothpicks to represent flags.

Separate black licorice pieces; use for doors, windows and so on.

Place fondant from centre of sweet on toothpick to represent a flag.

HOW TO MAKE EYELASHES
Using the licorice which comes in three strands, gently separate one strand from the other two strands. Using sharp-pointed scissors, make diagonal cuts in licorice about 3mm (⅛in) apart, do not cut right through. Cut to length required for eyelashes — about 5cm (2in) — bend into shape when positioning on cake.

Make diagonal cuts in licorice about 3mm (⅛in) apart for long eyelashes.

PIPED DECORATIONS
Some cakes require very simple piped decorations which can be done with a paper bag (see page 4). For those which use piped "stars", such as the Icecream Dolly Varden, a piping set is necessary. These are available ▷

BEFORE YOU START...

▷ from kitchenware sections of chain stores and hardware stores. The Formac piping set comes in two sizes: with nylon icing bag and six pipes for around $3.50 or with eight pipes for around $5.50. Each kit contains a screw attachment which fits into the end of the bag, holding tube in place; this makes it easy to change tubes.

PIPING WITH A PAPER BAG

Paper bags can be used for piping whipped cream, Royal Icing, Vienna Cream or Fluffy Frosting. Drop two heaped teaspoons of mixture into bag, try to avoid spreading mixture around open end. Gently ease mixture towards point of bag, fold over ends to secure top, as shown.

Using sharp scissors, snip 3mm (⅛in) from point of bag, then pipe a trail of icing; if a larger trail is needed, cut a fraction more from bag, then try piping again. In this way, just the right-sized trail will be obtained.

When piping, hold the paper bag with right hand so the folded-over section is secure, otherwise the mixture will come out of the top of the bag; use left hand to guide the bag as you pipe. Hold bag at a 45 degree angle, apply a little pressure with right hand for piping. If lefthanded, reverse this procedure.

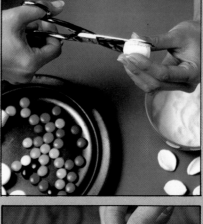

HOW TO MAKE PAPER PIPING BAGS

Cut out a square of greaseproof paper; it must have straight sides and each side must be of the same length to give a good-shaped bag for piping. Fold diagonally, cut into two triangles. Hold the apex of the triangle in your left hand with the point of the apex towards you, take the righthand point in your right hand, curl point of paper over until you have this point and the point of the apex touching; hold these two points with right hand. With left hand and left point of paper, wrap the paper over the top and halfway under the cone so this point meets the other two points exactly. (Of course, if you're lefthanded, reverse the procedure.) If the triangle is evenly cut, the three points will all touch and the cone shape will not have a hole at the tip.

Secure joins of bag, inside and out, with a piece of sticky tape. Always place the icing or cream used for piping in the bag first, then snip a tiny hole in the tip of the bag, gently push icing down, fold over ends to prevent icing coming out the top, enlarge hole with scissors to the required size (for more information, see Piping With A Paper Bag, this page).

HOW TO MAKE MARSHMALLOW FLOWERS

Using sharp scissors, cut each marshmallow in half horizontally, dip cut edges in castor sugar to prevent sticking. Cut halved marshmallows again into halves horizontally to give four petals from each marshmallow, dip cut edges in sugar. Press pointed tips of the four petals together to resemble a flower. Press a round flat sweet in centre of flower to cover join where the petals meet. For added colour, dip inside of each petal in coloured jelly crystals, as shown, before joining together to form flower.

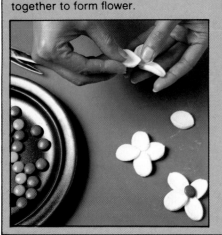

DOLLY VARDEN TINS

These are available at most kitchenware or department stores. However, if you have difficulty in obtaining one, write to: A. E. Westernhagen, 22 Addison Road, Marrickville, NSW 2204. This company manufactures the tins and can tell you the nearest stockist or they will send the tins by mail.

CUP AND SPOON MEASURES

Recipes in this book use the following standard metric equipment which has been approved by the Australian Standards Association:

(a) 250 millilitre cup for measuring liquids. A litre jug (capacity 4 cups) also is available.

(b) a graduated set of four cups measuring 1 cup, ½, ⅓ and ¼ cup for measuring items such as flour and sugar. When measuring in these fractional cups, level off at the brim.

(c) a graduated set of four spoons: tablespoon (20 millilitre liquid capacity), teaspoon (5 millilitre), ½ teaspoon and ¼ teaspoon.

Note: All spoon measurements mentioned in this book are level.

This metric equipment is approved by Australian Standards Association.

PREPARING BOARDS

To make the birthday cake easy to handle and attractive, place cake on a board which has been covered with decorative paper. The paper should have a greaseproof surface to prevent butter from the Vienna Cream being absorbed; aluminium foil is ideal and it can be bought in pretty patterns.

A flat piece of board is necessary (some of the smaller cakes can be placed on a plate or tray of suitable size and shape); a covered bread board or chopping board also can be used. If a special shape or size of board is required, Masonite cut to size can be used. Off-cuts are available in most large hardware stores.

Boards should be about 5cm (2in) larger all round than the cake. Individual recipes will indicate if a board of special size or shape is needed. Cake boards of wood or heavy cardboard can be bought from some health food stores, cake shops and shops which specialize in cake-decorating needs.

COVERING A SQUARE BOARD

Place paper, pattern side down, on a bench. Position board on paper, mark all the way around the board with a pencil. Remove board, cut out a square 2.5cm (1in) larger than the marked square. Using sharp scissors, cut out a piece from each corner, as shown, to avoid bulky corners; only cut to within 3mm (⅛in) of point of board. Place board in position, fold over the sides, secure paper with sticky tape.

COVERING A ROUND BOARD

Place paper, pattern side down, on a bench. Position board on paper, mark all the way around the board with a pencil. Remove board, cut out a circle 2.5cm (1in) larger than the marked circle. Using sharp scissors, make diagonal cuts about 2cm (¾in) apart around the border, cut to within 3mm (⅛in) of marked circle. Place board in position, fold over cut border, one piece at a time, secure paper with sticky tape.

Cut out pieces to avoid bulky corners.

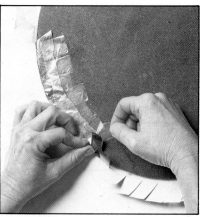

Secure the border with sticky tape.

OVEN TEMPERATURES

ELECTRIC TEMPERATURES	FAHRENHEIT	CELSIUS
Very slow	250	120
Slow	300	150
Moderately slow	325-350	160-180
Moderate	375-400	190-200
Moderately hot	425-450	220-230
Hot	475-500	250-260
Very hot	525-550	270-290

GAS TEMPERATURES	FAHRENHEIT	CELSIUS
Very slow	250	120
Slow	275-300	140-150
Moderately slow	325	160
Moderate	350	180
Moderately hot	375	190
Hot	400-450	200-230
Very hot	475-500	250-260

STORYBOOK FAVOURITES

HICKORY DICKORY WATCH

1 packet butter cake mix
1 quantity Vienna Cream
hundreds and thousands
licorice
assorted round jubes
1 toothpick
1 prune
musk lollies or almond pieces

Make cake according to directions on packet, pour into greased deep 20cm (8in) round cake tin, bake in moderate oven 50 minutes or until cooked when tested. Turn on to wire rack to cool, then place on prepared board.

If desired, tint Vienna Cream with a few drops yellow food colouring. With a knife dipped in hot water, spread Vienna Cream evenly over cake. Place 15cm (6in) diameter saucepan lid on top of cake, coat exposed top and sides with hundreds and thousands, remove saucepan lid carefully. Make numerals, clock hands and mouse tail from licorice, place numerals and hands in position, use coloured jube for centre.

Press coloured jubes around edge of clock face. Make winder by pressing two jubes on to a toothpick, press into clock. A prune with licorice piece for tail, small musks or almond pieces for eyes represents the mouse.

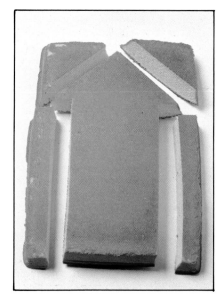

HICKORY DICKORY DOCK

1 packet butter cake mix
1 quantity Vienna Cream
red food colouring
1 tablespoon cocoa
1 tablespoon water
assorted sweets (as shown)
licorice
2 prunes
jelly snakes

Make cake according to directions on packet, spoon evenly into greased 28cm x 18cm (11in x 7in) lamington tin, bake in moderate oven 30 minutes or until cooked when tested. Turn on to wire rack to cool.

Cut out cake, as shown. Using a 9cm (3½in) round cutter as a guide, mark a circle on top of cake to represent face of clock; place cake on prepared board. Place a quarter of Vienna Cream in small bowl, tint pink with a few drops red food colouring. Combine cocoa and water, colour remaining Vienna Cream with cocoa mixture. Spread pink Vienna Cream evenly over face of clock, continue down body of cake to within 4cm (1½in) in from edges of cake, as shown, spread chocolate Vienna Cream evenly over rest of cake. Decorate edges with small sweets, outline pink section with small sweets.

Place small amount of chocolate Vienna Cream in corner of small paper bag (see page 4), pipe numbers on face of clock. Thin strips of licorice represent the hands of the clock; thin strips of licorice and flat round sweets represent the pendulums. Decorate the prunes to represent mice; we used round sweets halved for the ears, thin strips of licorice for tails and thin strips of jelly snakes for whiskers.

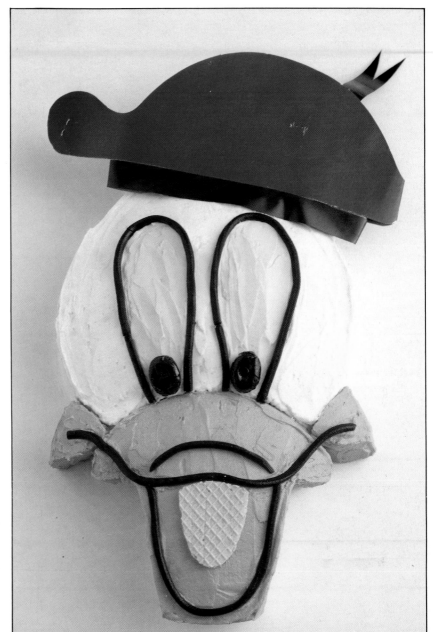

DONALD DUCK *

2 packets butter cake mix
1 quantity Vienna Cream
yellow food colouring
red food colouring
blue food colouring
licorice strips
1 icecream wafer
2 large sweets
party hat
black Sasheen ribbon

Make cakes according to directions on packet, pour just over half into greased deep 23cm (9in) round cake tin, pour remainder into greased deep 20cm (8in) round cake tin, so that both mixtures are the same depth, bake in moderate oven 45 minutes or until cooked when tested. Turn cakes on to wire racks to cool.

Cut out bill and mouth from large cake, as shown. Cut a small arc from smaller cake so that top of mouth fits in snugly, as shown in reconstructed picture. Cut ends off piece from arc, place one on either side of mouth to form the bill, as shown in reconstructed picture. Assemble, as shown, on prepared board. Divide cream in half; tint one half orange using a combination of yellow and red food colourings. Ice mouth and bill with the orange cream. Ice head with white Vienna Cream, leaving an area for the eyes.

Tint remaining cream pale blue with food colouring, spread over eye area. Outline eyes and mouth with thin strips of licorice. Cut tongue from icecream wafer and place in position. Place sweets in lower parts of eyes. Select hat from packet of children's party hats, available at department stores and newsagencies, decorate with black gift-wrapping ribbon.

*Copyright © Walt Disney Productions.

MICKEY MOUSE *

2 packets butter cake mix
1 quantity Vienna Cream
pink food colouring
chocolate sprinkles
wooden skewer
1 pink icecream wafer
1 oval chocolate biscuit
2 small brown sweets
licorice
ribbon

Make cakes according to directions on packet, pour just over half into greased deep 23cm (9in) round cake tin, pour the rest into greased deep 20cm (8in) round cake tin, so that both mixtures are the same depth, bake in moderate oven 45 minutes or until cooked when tested. Turn on to wire racks to cool.

Using a large pastry cutter or small bowl 10cm (4in) in diameter, cut out two circles from 20cm (8in) cake to make the ears. Cut trimmings to form extended jawline. Cut 23cm (9in) cake and assemble, as shown, on prepared board. Reserve 2 tablespoons of Vienna Cream, tint remaining cream pale pink with food colouring. Cover top and sides of cake with pink cream, leaving a small area for eyes; cover eye area with reserved white cream. Coat top and sides of the ears and the head with chocolate sprinkles.

Using a skewer, draw shape of mouth in icing then fill in carefully with chocolate sprinkles. Cut icecream wafer into shape of tongue, place in position. Place chocolate biscuit in centre of cake to form the nose. Place chocolate sweets in corners of eyes. Use licorice strips for eyebrows and nose. Tie ribbon into large bow, secure at base of cake.

MINNIE MOUSE *

2 packets butter cake mix
1 quantity Vienna Cream
pink food colouring
chocolate sprinkles
licorice
1 pink icecream wafer
1 large red sweet for nose
2 large sweets for eyes
ribbon
paper doyley

Make cakes according to directions on packet, pour just over half into greased deep 23cm (9in) round cake tin, pour the rest into greased deep 20cm (8in) round cake tin, so that both mixtures are the same depth, bake in moderate oven 45 minutes or until cooked when tested. Turn on to wire racks to cool.

Using a large pastry cutter or small bowl about 10cm (4in) in diameter, cut two circles from 20cm (8in) cake to make the ears. Cut trimmings to form extended jawline, as for Mickey Mouse. Cut 23cm (9in) cake, as shown in picture. Assemble cake, as shown, on prepared board. Reserve 2 tablespoons Vienna Cream, tint remaining cream pale pink with a few drops food colouring, cover top and sides with pink cream, leaving a small area for eyes, cover eye area with reserved white cream. Coat top and sides of ears and head with chocolate sprinkles, as shown.

Using thin strips of licorice, outline the mouth. Trim short lengths of licorice with scissors to form eyelashes. Cut icecream wafer into shape of tongue, place in position. Place nose and eyes in position. Tie ribbon into large bow, place on top of head between ears. Fold doyley in half, cut out centre, place around neck for collar.

*Copyright © Walt Disney Productions.

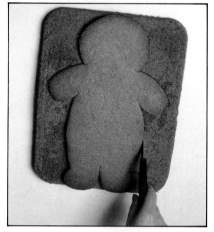

GINGERBREAD MAN

BISCUIT
1¼ tablespoons golden syrup
60g (2oz) butter
¼ cup sugar
1 egg yolk
1¼ cups plain flour
½ teaspoon bicarbonate of soda
1½ teaspoons ground ginger

CAKE
1 packet chocolate butter cake mix
½ quantity chocolate Vienna Cream
chocolate sprinkles
⅓ cup apricot jam
round flat sweets
licorice
2 marshmallows
small sweet for nose
1 board 40cm x 35cm (16in x 14in)

ROYAL ICING
1 egg white
1¼ to 1½ cups icing sugar

Biscuit: Pour golden syrup into small heatproof jug, stand jug in heatproof dish or saucepan of hot water until syrup warms and softens. Cream the butter and sugar until light and fluffy, add egg yolk, beat well; slowly add sifted dry ingredients and warmed syrup, mix well. Knead mixture lightly.

Roll out on to very lightly greased oven tray to size of gingerbread man outline, trace outline on to grease-proof paper, cut out pattern, place on dough, cut around paper pattern with a sharp knife. Bake in moderate oven 20 minutes or until cooked. Allow to cool on oven tray. (Make gingerbread biscuits with leftover mixture.)

Cake: Make cake according to directions on packet, pour into greased 30cm x 25cm (12in x 10in) swiss roll tin, bake in moderate oven 20 minutes or until cooked when tested. Turn on to wire rack to cool. Place chocolate cake on board, place gingerbread man biscuit on top of cake. With a sharp knife, cut cake to shape of gingerbread man, cover sides with chocolate Vienna Cream, coat thickly with chocolate sprinkles. Heat jam, push through fine sieve, brush gingerbread man lightly and evenly with jam to give a glaze. Decorate gingerbread man with flat round sweets for buttons, licorice for mouth, halved marshmallows topped with halved round sweets for eyes, small sweet for nose.

Royal Icing: Using a wooden spoon, beat egg white lightly in small bowl, add sifted icing sugar 1 tablespoon at a time, beating well after each addition until icing stands in firm peaks (amount of icing sugar required depends on size of egg white). Fill paper bag (see page 4) with Royal Icing, pipe decoratively around edge of gingerbread man, pipe a dot on each button.

PATTERN FOR GINGERBREAD MAN

HUMPTY DUMPTY
CAKE
1 packet butter cake mix
1 quantity chocolate Vienna Cream
1 empty matchbox
cocoa
green jelly snakes
assorted sweets (as shown)
coconut
green food colouring
HUMPTY DUMPTY
1 egg
scraps coloured cardboard
scraps fabric
pipecleaners
oil paints or felt-tipped pens

Cake: Make cake according to directions on packet, pour into greased 20cm x 10cm (8in x 4in) loaf tin, bake in moderate oven 50 minutes or until cooked when tested. Turn on to wire rack to cool.

When cold, trim top so cake will sit flat, place upside down on prepared board, spread evenly with Vienna Cream. Tear paper from end of matchbox cover, remove striker sides, dip end in cocoa, shake off excess, mark bricks on wall with matchbox end, as shown. Decorate with flowers made from coloured sweets, using green jelly snakes for stems. Make path with chocolate sweets and coloured sweets. Green-tinted coconut represents grass.

Humpty Dumpty: Remove centre from egg by piercing with pin at either end, then blowing contents out of shell. Or egg can be boiled until hard. Make clothing from scraps coloured cardboard or fabric, legs and arms from cardboard or pipecleaners, hat from cardboard. Paint or draw face, hair and moustache with oil paints or felt-tipped pens.

14

MISS MUFFET

1 packet butter cake mix
1 quantity Vienna Cream
pink food colouring
2 tablespoons cocoa
chocolate sprinkles
2 soft sweets
4 pipecleaners
small doll

Make cake according to directions on packet, place 1 tablespoon in paper patty case in deep patty pan (this cake is for Miss Muffet's stool), spread remaining mixture into greased deep 20cm (8in) cake tin, bake in moderate oven 10 to 15 minutes for stool, 50 minutes for the large cake or until cooked when tested. Turn cake on to wire rack to cool.

Trim tops of cakes so they are flat. Remove 1 tablespoon of the Vienna Cream, tint pink with a drop of food colouring, add sifted cocoa to remaining cream, mix well. Spread sides of patty cake with chocolate cream, roll in chocolate sprinkles. (Do not put cream on seat of stool; butter in the cream will mark the doll's dress.) Spread cream around sides of large cake; hold cake top and bottom between two hands, roll in chocolate sprinkles. Place large cake on prepared board, spread top evenly with more cream.

Make web with the pink cream by piping a cross on the cake, then dividing the cross into eight, as shown. Finish piping web, starting from the centre. Choose two colourful soft sweets for the spider, cut pipecleaners in half, bend to shape of spider's legs, insert ends into body of spider. Place spider on cake, join head to body with a little Vienna Cream, pipe eyes with pink cream. Place stool near large cake, position doll on stool.

OLD WOMAN WHO LIVED IN A SHOE

3 packets butter cake mix
1 wooden skewer
1½ quantities chocolate
    Vienna Cream
icecream wafers
licorice allsorts
licorice
assorted sweets (as shown)
chocolate-coated sultanas
Lifesavers
toothpicks
1 board 38cm (15in) square

Make cakes according to directions on packet, spoon one third into greased 2 litre (8 cup) pudding basin, spoon remainder of mixture evenly into two greased 23cm x 12cm (9in x 5in) loaf tins, bake in moderate oven 55 to 60 minutes for pudding basin, 50 minutes for loaf tins or until cooked when tested. Turn cakes on to wire rack to cool.

Cut 5mm (¼in) slice off one end of pudding basin cake (cut-off piece forms heel of shoe, the rest forms toe),

stand loaf cakes upright behind toe, as shown; if necessary, trim sides and tops of loaf cakes to make them even. Place heel in position, stick a long wooden skewer through heel to toe to hold pieces in position. Cut a curve in top end of cake directly behind toe, as shown, to form shoe opening. Cut a curve out of base of same cake, as shown, to form arch of shoe.

Cover cake completely with Vienna Cream, place icecream wafers on top of cake to form roof. Cut licorice allsorts in half lengthwise, place narrow strips licorice across centres, press allsorts around cake to form windows. Cut shutters from icecream wafers, place on either side of windows. Make door from small sweets, path from chocolate-coated sultanas. Lifesavers represent eyelets; join with licorice strips to make laces, press licorice bow above laces. For flowers, press toothpicks into round jubes, then press coloured soft sweets on other ends. Back window is made with icecream wafers and small sweets.

GINGERBREAD HOUSE

2 packets gingerbread cake mix
toothpicks
1 quantity chocolate Vienna Cream
small assorted sweets (as shown)
licorice
1 icecream wafer
2 chocolate biscuit sticks
chocolate-coated sultanas
coconut
green food colouring

Make up one cake mix as directed on packet, pour into greased 23cm x 12cm (9in x 5in) loaf tin, bake in moderate oven 50 minutes or until cooked when tested. Make up second cake mix as directed on packet, pour half the mixture into greased 25cm x 8cm (10in x 3in) bar tin, bake in moderate oven 30 minutes or until cooked when tested. Pour remaining cake mixture into greased patty tins to make extra patty cakes for future use, bake in moderate oven 10 to 15 minutes or until cooked when tested. Turn on to wire racks to cool. Cut bar cake in half horizontally, join together at top with toothpicks, place on top of loaf cake to form roof, as shown.

Spread chocolate Vienna Cream evenly and smoothly all over cake. Overlap sweets on roof to represent tiles, press licorice log along top of roof tiles. Use wafer for door and sweet for door knob, secure with small stick. Use large sweets for windows and halved jubes for frames. Secure small sweets and leaves with small sticks to chocolate biscuit sticks to represent flower beds. Use chocolate sultanas for path. Tint coconut with a few drops green food colouring, sprinkle over board to represent grass.

PATTERN FOR PUSS IN BOOTS

PUSS IN BOOTS
2 packets butter cake mix
greaseproof paper
1 quantity Vienna Cream
green food colouring
apricot food colouring
thin licorice
tubular licorice
2 round green sweets
2 red glace cherries
1 toothpick
1 board 50cm x 40cm (20in x 16in)
Make cakes according to directions on packet, divide evenly between two greased 28cm x 18cm (11in x 7in) lamington tins, bake in moderate oven 30 minutes or until cooked when tested. Turn on to wire racks to cool.

Place cakes side by side, trim long sides so the two cakes fit tightly together. Trace patterns on to greaseproof paper, cut out, pin on top of cakes, as shown, with a small sharp serrated knife, cut out cake using pattern as guide. Assemble on board.

Tint half Vienna Cream with green food colouring, tint other half with apricot food colouring, ice hat and boots with green Vienna Cream, as shown, ice rest of cake with apricot Vienna Cream, as shown. Outline cake and define leg with thin licorice strips, as shown; split tubular licorice lengthwise, press out flat, cut nose and paw pads from licorice, position, as shown; cut whiskers, eyebrows, mouth and claws out of thin licorice strips, place in position. Round green sweets represent eyes, halved glace cherry represents tongue, whole glace cherry secured with toothpick to tip of hat represents pompom.

19

SPORT

SOCCER BALL
2 packets butter cake mix
1 quantity Vienna Cream
cocoa
licorice
coconut
green food colouring
Make cakes according to directions on packet, divide evenly and pour into two well-greased 2 litre (8 cup) pudding steamers, bake in moderate oven 60 minutes or until cooked when tested. Turn on to wire rack to cool. When cold, invert each cake, trim tops so that they will sit flat.

Place one cake narrow side down on prepared board, place other cake on top of this; join them with a little Vienna Cream. With serrated knife, trim cakes to give round shape. Cover with Vienna Cream, mark hexagonal shapes lightly on icing using tracing wheel dipped in cocoa. Make eyelets for laces from rounds of licorice pressed into shape with fingers; use licorice strips for laces. Surround ball with green-tinted coconut to represent grass.

CRICKET PITCH

1 packet butter cake mix
1 quantity Vienna Cream
1 tablespoon cocoa
green food colouring
**2 x 150g packets chocolate
  biscuit sticks**
coconut
bamboo skewers
red nailpolish
wooden iceblock stick
small wooden stick
small round red sweet
white toothpaste

Make cake according to directions on packet, spoon into greased deep 20cm (8in) round cake tin, bake in moderate oven 50 minutes or until cooked when tested. Turn on to wire rack to cool. Trim 1cm (½in) off top of cake to make the cake lower than the chocolate biscuit sticks so that they will stand up around it like a fence.

Combine 2 tablespoons of the Vienna Cream with 1 tablespoon sifted cocoa, mix well. Mark a rectangle in the centre of the cake 4cm x 9cm (1½in x 3½in), spread chocolate cream evenly inside rectangle. Tint remaining Vienna Cream with green food colouring, spread evenly over remaining cake. Arrange chocolate sticks around edge, cover top with green-tinted coconut (be careful not to get coconut over chocolate cream).

Cut bamboo skewers into six 5cm (2in) lengths, paint with red nailpolish; do not paint at end where sticks go into cake. When dry, arrange three sticks side by side at each end of pitch to represent stumps. Cut two pieces of bamboo skewers to fit across top of stumps, paint with nailpolish, place on the stumps.

Trim wooden iceblock stick with scissors to bat shape. For handle of bat, position small wooden stick on back of bat with Vienna Cream. Use a small round red sweet for ball; paint white line around centre of ball with brush dipped in toothpaste.

SWIMMING POOL

1 packet butter cake mix
100g packet lime jelly crystals
1 quantity chocolate Vienna Cream
2 x 150g packets chocolate
  biscuit sticks
2 musk sticks
licorice
assorted food colourings
assorted round sweets
small dolls
jube rings
green sprinkles
nailpolish
jelly snakes
small paper umbrella

Make cake according to directions on packet, spoon evenly into greased deep 20cm (8in) round cake tin, bake in moderate oven 50 minutes or until cooked when tested. Turn cake on to wire rack to cool. Make up jelly as directed on packet; refrigerate until it is set.

Trim top of cake so that it is flat; cut around top about 1cm (½in) in from edge to represent wall of swimming pool. Using small sharp knife, hollow out centre of cake, as shown, to 2.5cm (1in) deep to form a recess for the jelly.

Spread sides and edge of cake with chocolate Vienna Cream. Arrange chocolate biscuit sticks evenly around cake, leaving an opening of about 5cm (2in). Use musk sticks and licorice to make ladder. Mash set jelly with fork, spoon into the recess of the cake to represent water.

Paint stripes of food colouring on to small round sweets to represent beach balls. Small dolls can be pushed through jube rings to represent children in rubber floats. Spread a little cream on heads of dolls, dip in green sprinkles (these represent bathing caps). Bathing suits can be painted on dolls with nailpolish. Rubber mattress is made from jelly snakes trimmed to about 5cm (2in) and joined together with a little chocolate cream. Add paper umbrella, as shown.

CRICKET BAT

2 packets butter cake mix
1 tablespoon instant coffee powder
1 tablespoon boiling water
1½ quantities Vienna Cream
60g (2oz) dark chocolate
green food colouring
coconut
ping pong ball
red nail polish
black felt-tipped pen
1 board 50cm x 25cm (20in x 10in)

Make cakes according to directions on packet, divide evenly and pour into two 28cm x 18cm (11in x 7in) greased lamington tins, bake in moderate oven 30 minutes or until cooked when tested. Turn on to wire rack to cool. Trim both cakes all round. Cut cakes, as shown in first picture; the two centre pieces form the bat. From one remaining piece of cake, cut a wedge approximately 25cm (10in) long.

Assemble cake on prepared board, as shown, with long wedge positioned down centre of bat. Taper off ends of wedge, as shown, to give bat a slightly raised effect in the centre.

Dissolve coffee powder in boiling water, cool; add to Vienna Cream, beat until smooth. Spread cake completely with coffee Vienna Cream, mark shape of handle, cover handle with grated chocolate. Cover the board with green-tinted coconut. Ping pong ball painted red and marked with black stitching represents the cricket ball.

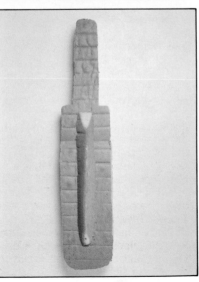

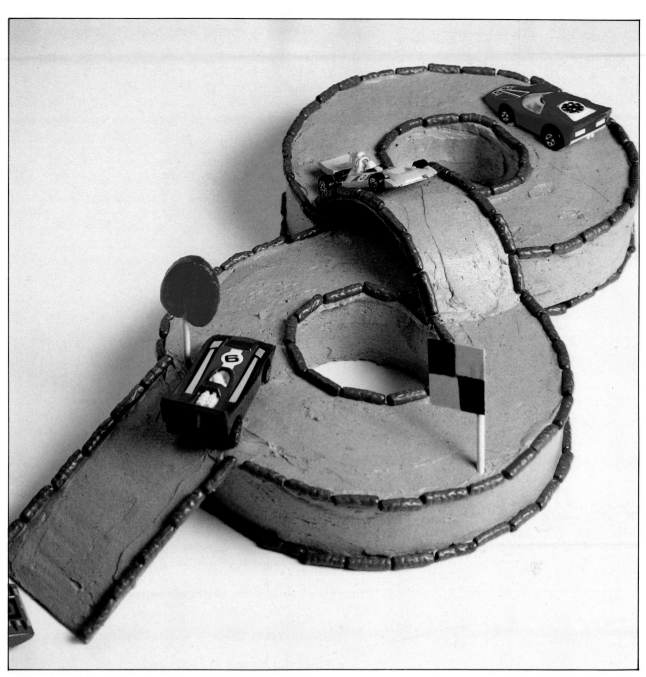

RACING TRACK

1 packet butter cake mix
2 quantities chocolate
   Vienna Cream
sweets for decoration
cardboard
small lollipop
toy racing cars
1 board 50cm x 30cm (20in x 12in)

Make cake according to directions on packet, pour into greased 20cm (8in) ring tin, bake in moderate oven 35 minutes or until cooked when tested. Turn on to wire rack to cool.

Cut cake in half horizontally, then cut small piece from one end of each circle, as shown; this helps the two halves fit neatly together in a figure eight. Discard the cut-off pieces. Assemble cake on prepared board.

Cover cakes with Vienna Cream, decorate edges of track with small sweets. Cut two strips of cardboard, about 15cm x 6cm (6in x 2½in), to represent bridge and ramp. Cover strips of cardboard with Vienna Cream. Place on cake, outline with small sweets, as shown. Place small lollipop on cake to represent stop sign. Make flag from cardboard, stand in cake. Arrange racing cars on track, as shown.

FOOTBALL

2 packets butter cake mix
1 quantity chocolate Vienna Cream
cocoa
licorice
green food colouring
coconut

Make cakes according to directions on packet, divide evenly between two well-greased Dolly Varden cake tins (see note), bake in moderate oven 1 hour or until cooked when tested. Turn cakes on to wire racks to cool. (If you only have one Dolly Varden cake tin, you can bake the cakes one at a time.)

Trim broad ends of cakes so they sit flat; trim small piece from underside of each so they do not roll over when being iced. Join cakes, broad ends together, with a little Vienna Cream; place on prepared board, cover cakes completely with the cream. Mark in stitching using tracing wheel dipped in cocoa. Make eyelets with small pieces of licorice pressed into rounds with fingers; make laces and numbers with licorice strips. Surround with green-tinted coconut.

Note: Dolly Varden cake tins are sold in large department stores and shops specializing in cake-decorating equipment (see note on Dolly Varden tins, page 5). If these tins are unavailable, you can use two 2 litre (8 cup) pudding steamers but, if these are used, the cakes will need a lot of trimming to the required shape and the cake will be quite small.

TENNIS RACQUET

2 packets butter cake mix
2 tablespoons cocoa
1 quantity Vienna Cream
1 tablespoon instant coffee powder
2 teaspoons boiling water
22 x 25cm (10in) bamboo skewers
assorted small sweets
1 board 55cm x 30cm (22in x 12in)

Make up cakes according to directions on packet, pour three quarters of combined mixture into greased 30cm x 25cm (12in x 10in) swiss roll tin and remaining quarter into greased 25cm x 8cm (10in x 3in) bar tin, bake in moderate oven 20 to 30 minutes or until cooked when tested. Turn on to wire racks to cool.

Cut large oval from swiss roll cake, as shown. Trim sides of bar tin cake to make 25cm x 4cm (10in x 1½in) rectangle, as shown, to form handle. Cut small semicircle at one end of bar cake to form top curve of handle. Cut around shape of oval about 1cm (½in) in from edge to

make frame of racquet. Using a small sharp knife, cut out centre of oval leaving 1cm (½in) of cake on base.

Add sifted cocoa to a quarter of the Vienna Cream, beat until well combined. Dissolve coffee in the water, cool; add to remaining Vienna Cream, beat until combined. Put oval on to covered board, cover recess in cake and inside rim with coffee-flavoured Vienna Cream. Push bamboo skewers across cake at 1cm (½in) intervals; do the same along the length of the racquet to make the strings. Trim ends of skewers if necessary. Cover frame and sides of racquet with chocolate Vienna Cream. Ice handle with coffee Vienna Cream. Secure handle to racquet with Vienna Cream. Cover join with small sweets. Decorate sides of handle and racquet with small sweets, as shown.

Note: Bamboo skewers are available at most supermarkets and Chinese food stores.

RUGBY FIELD

AUSSIE RULES FIELD

SOCCER FIELD

ROYAL ICING
1 egg white
1 to 1¼ cups pure icing sugar
CAKE
1 packet butter cake mix
1 quantity Vienna Cream
green food colouring
coconut
small round red sweet
white pipecleaners
small piece net
licorice allsorts

Royal Icing: Beat egg white lightly, add the sifted icing sugar, one dessertspoon at a time; beat well after each addition until icing forms peaks.

Cake: Make the cake according to directions on packet. Spoon evenly into greased 28cm x 18cm (11in x 7in) lamington tin, bake in moderate oven 30 to 35 minutes or until cooked when tested. Turn on to wire rack to cool. Tint Vienna Cream with a few drops of green food colouring, ice cake evenly, cover with green-tinted coconut. Mark the lines on the cake with ruler. Mark the circle and half circles with scone cutter. Spoon the Royal Icing into one corner of a small paper bag (see page 4). Pipe lines in grooves on cake, as shown. Pipe triangles of Royal Icing on a small round red sweet to represent the soccer ball; place on cake.

Make goal posts from white pipecleaners, insert in cake, twist into shape, as shown. Cut piece of cotton net (or bag used for onions) to fit over posts, as shown. Make crosspieces for goal posts from small pieces of pipecleaner, thread net on to pipecleaner, position on posts, as shown, twist ends under to secure. Insert small piece pipecleaner in cake as a peg to hold net in place; coconut will hold sides of net down. Make flags from licorice allsorts (see page 3).

RUGBY FIELD

Make up cake as above, using picture as guide. Goal posts are made from bamboo skewers glued together and painted white with shoe cleaner. A chocolate-coated almond represents the football.

Note: The ends of skewers which go into cake should not be painted.

AUSSIE RULES FIELD

Make up cake as above, cut into oval shape and continue as above. Pipe lines on to cake, using picture as guide. Goal posts are made from bamboo skewers; the four larger middle posts are painted white with shoe cleaner, while the four smaller outside posts are painted red with nailpolish. A chocolate-coated "clinker" sweet, striped with red nailpolish, represents the football.

Note: The ends of skewers which go into cake should not be painted.

ANIMALS

BROWN BEAR

2 packets butter cake mix
1 quantity Vienna Cream
3 tablespoons cocoa
250g (8oz) coconut
brown food colouring
2 Wagon Wheel biscuits
assorted sweets (as shown)
licorice
1 board 58cm x 45cm (23in x 18in)

Make cakes according to directions on packet, pour half into greased deep 20cm (8in) round cake tin, pour other half into greased deep 23cm (9in) square cake tin, bake in moderate oven 45 minutes for square cake, 50 minutes for round cake or until cooked when tested. Turn on to wire rack to cool.

Cut square cake, as shown; assemble cake, as shown, on prepared board, using cut-out pieces for paws. Leave 3 tablespoons Vienna Cream plain, stir sifted cocoa into remaining Vienna Cream. Spread plain Vienna Cream over tummy and face, cover top and sides of rest of cake with chocolate Vienna Cream. Leave ¾ cup coconut plain, tint remainder with brown food colouring, sprinkle brown coconut over brown icing, sprinkle plain coconut over tummy and part of face, as shown. Cover top and sides of paws with plain Vienna Cream, then coat with plain coconut, place paws in position. Wagon Wheels represent ears, assorted sweets represent features on face, tummy and paws, a thin licorice strip represents mouth.

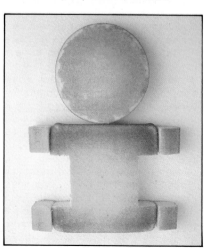

31

SMILEY SHARK
2 packets butter cake mix
1 quantity Vienna Cream
green food colouring
2 small round sweets
licorice
small white peppermints
hundreds and thousands
1 board 60cm x 30cm (24in x 12in)
Make cakes according to directions on packet, divide evenly between two greased 25cm x 15cm (10in x 6in) loaf tins, bake in moderate oven 45 minutes or until cooked when tested. Turn on to wire rack to cool. (Use cakes top side up to give rounded appearance to shark's body.)

Cut slice off end of each cake so they can be joined end to end, as shown. Make head by rounding end of cake with small sharp serrated knife, cut tail to shape, as shown; retain all scraps of cake. Trim body to rounded shape, as shown, cut dorsal fin from one large scrap, cut other fins and tail pieces from the remaining scraps. Tint Vienna Cream with a few drops green food colouring, place body of shark on prepared board, join pieces with a little Vienna Cream. Cut a slender wedge, about 5cm (2in) deep, from head to make mouth, trim lower jaw so it is about 1cm (½in) smaller than upper jaw. Spread body with Vienna Cream. Small round sweets represent eyes, licorice cut to shape represents eyelashes (see page 3), halved peppermints such as Tic Tacs represent teeth. Spread fins and tail pieces with Vienna Cream, roll in hundreds and thousands, position, as shown (dorsal fin goes on top of body). Tail pieces and dorsal fin may need to be held in place with thin bamboo skewers pushed right through to the board for maximum stability.

Note: Decorate cake on day of serving; if decorated beforehand, the Vienna Cream will cause the hundreds and thousands to soften and the colour will run into the Vienna Cream.

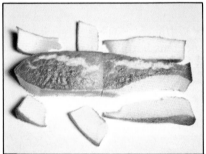

LITTLE PIGGY

1 packet butter cake mix
1 quantity Vienna Cream
red food colouring
assorted sweets (as shown)
marshmallow flowers (see page 4)

Make cake according to directions on packet, divide evenly, pour into two greased 20cm (8in) round sandwich tins, bake in moderate oven 25 minutes or until cooked when tested. Turn on to wire rack to cool.

Using 15cm (6in) saucer as guide, cut one cake, as shown; cut out nose with 5cm (2in) plain cutter; cut both side pieces into two to make feet. To assemble, place head on top of second cake, position nose, position feet, as shown, on prepared board.

Tint Vienna Cream with a few drops red food colouring, cover cakes with Vienna Cream. Jelly snakes represent hair and tail, thin licorice with diagonal slits cut out represents eyelashes (see page 3), jubes or coloured sweets represent eyes. Decorate with marshmallow flowers.

TOMMY TURTLE, LUCY LADYBIRD AND SAMMY SNAIL

1 packet butter cake mix
1 quantity Vienna Cream

TOMMY TURTLE
thick licorice
1 tablespoon cocoa
green food colouring
1 glace cherry

LUCY LADYBIRD
1 tablespoon cocoa
orange food colouring
round flat brown sweets
1 pipecleaner
2 red sweets for eyes

SAMMY SNAIL
1 tablespoon cocoa
yellow food colouring
1 pipecleaner
silver cachous

You will need patty cakes for each of these cakes: three for the turtle, two each for the snail or ladybird. Make cake according to directions on packet, drop 1 tablespoon mixture into each paper patty case in deep patty pans, spread remaining mixture into greased 2 litre (8 cup) pudding basin, bake in moderate oven 10 to 15 minutes for patty cakes, 1 hour for large cake or until cooked when tested. Turn on to wire rack to cool.

Tommy Turtle: Use one patty cake for head, cut remaining two patty cakes in half vertically for feet, position cakes, as shown. Shape piece of thick licorice for tail, place in position. Add 1 tablespoon sifted cocoa to ⅓ cup Vienna Cream, mix well; tint remaining Vienna Cream with green food colouring, spread body of turtle with green Vienna Cream, mark in shell pattern with skewer; spread head, feet and tail with brown Vienna Cream, place in position, mark claws on feet with skewer, mark in mouth with skewer, a glace cherry cut into halves represents eyes.

Lucy Ladybird: Cut one patty cake in half vertically (only one piece is needed); cut other patty cake in half vertically, trim 1cm (½in) from ends, discard small pieces. Assemble, as shown, placing the two trimmed cakes end to end against the large cake; place one half of the other patty cake in position, as shown. Add 1 tablespoon sifted cocoa to ¼ cup Vienna Cream, mix well; tint remaining Vienna Cream with orange food colouring, spread orange Vienna Cream over ladybird's body, mark in wing division with skewer, add round flat brown sweets to represent spots; cover head parts with brown Vienna Cream. Small pieces of pipecleaner represent feelers, red sweets represent eyes.

Sammy Snail: Trim two patty cakes to cylindrical shape, cut one in half lengthwise. Make head with whole trimmed patty cake and half other cake, as shown; remaining half, trimmed to triangular shape, represents tail. Assemble, as shown. Add 1 tablespoon sifted cocoa to ¼ cup Vienna Cream, mix well; tint remaining Vienna Cream with yellow food colouring, spread yellow Vienna Cream over body of snail, mark in circular pattern with skewer, cover head and tail with brown Vienna Cream. Pieces of pipecleaner represent horns, silver cachou clusters represent eyes.

WISE OLD OWL
2 packets butter cake mix
pink food colouring
2 quantities Vienna Cream
3 tablespoons cocoa
3 cups coconut
brown food colouring
assorted sweets (as shown)
1 board 50cm x 30cm (20in x 12in)

Make cakes according to directions on packet, divide evenly, pour into two greased deep 20cm (8in) round cake tins, bake in moderate oven 50 minutes or until cooked when tested. Turn on to wire racks to cool.

Cut one cake, as shown; assemble on board. Add a few drops pink food colouring to a quarter of the Vienna Cream to tint it a pretty pink; add sifted cocoa to remaining Vienna Cream, mix well. Spread head and wings with chocolate Vienna Cream, spread body with pink-tinted Vienna Cream. Tint approximately 1½ cups coconut with a few drops brown food colouring, sprinkle over head and wings. Reserve ½ cup coconut, tint the rest with pink food colouring, sprinkle over body of owl. Make rings around eyes with plain coconut; black licorice rings represent eyes, a jube represents nose, licorice strips represent eyebrows, nose and feet.

PUSSYCAT
1 packet butter cake mix
1½ quantities chocolate
Vienna Cream
125g (4oz) dark chocolate
1 cup shredded coconut
½ cup desiccated coconut
pink food colouring
licorice
assorted sweets (as shown)
1 board 50cm x 30cm (20in x 12in)

Make cake according to directions on packet, pour just over half into greased 20cm (8in) sandwich tin, pour rest into greased 18cm (7in) sandwich tin, bake in moderate oven 30 minutes for the larger cake, 20 minutes for the smaller or until cooked when tested. Cool in tins 3 minutes, turn on to wire rack to cool.

Cut cakes, as shown; assemble on board, as shown. With spatula or knife, spread cakes evenly with chocolate Vienna Cream, mark out eyes and tummy, sprinkle grated chocolate over rest of face and body; mark eyes with desiccated coconut. Tint shredded coconut with a few drops pink food colouring, arrange over ears and centre of tummy. Cut licorice for whiskers and tail; black jelly beans represent eyes, marshmallows represent nose, jubes make necktie, as shown.

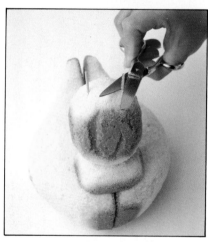

RUBBER DUCKY

2 packets butter cake mix
2 bamboo skewers
1 quantity Fluffy Frosting (2 egg
**   white quantity)**
apricot food colouring
round flat sweets (as shown)
licorice
coloured popcorn
potato crisps
wide ribbon

Make cakes according to directions on packet, pour one quarter of mixture into greased 25cm × 8cm (10in × 3in) bar tin, pour remaining mixture into greased deep 20cm (8in) square cake tin, bake in moderate oven 30 minutes for bar cake, 1 hour for square cake or until cooked when tested. Stand 3 minutes, turn on to wire rack to cool.

Cut square cake in half vertically, as shown; place bar cake on its side, cut in half, cut wedge-shaped piece off one end, as shown. Only the half with the wedge cut off is required; it forms the head and neck. Stand the two pieces of square cake side by side with cut sides up and bases together, cut off the four corners, cutting more from one end than the other, as shown, for the duck's tail end, then cut a wedge-shaped piece from tail end, as shown, to give shape to the body; discard scraps. Take the piece of bar cake for head and neck, cut four small wedges, one from each side, 2cm (¾in) in from end where wedge was cut; this angled end is where neck joins body.

Shape duck's body by making a cut at tail end: cut down on an angle for about 2.5cm (1in), then cut upwards, still on an angle, towards front of body; shape body carefully with small serrated knife to give rounded effect. Position head and neck piece, secure with two bamboo skewers, as shown, pushing skewers right through body. Shape head carefully with small serrated knife, so that neck sits neatly on body; cut off ends of skewers, as shown. It is necessary to leave skewers in place to support head.

Place duck on prepared board, tint Fluffy Frosting with apricot food colouring, cover head and body with Fluffy Frosting, leave sides looking fluffy to represent feathers, smooth head, neck and chest with a small spatula. Small coloured sweets represent eyes and buttons; surround eyes with thin strips of licorice. Yellow popcorn represents down on head, two large potato crisps represent bill. Place large bow at duck's neck.

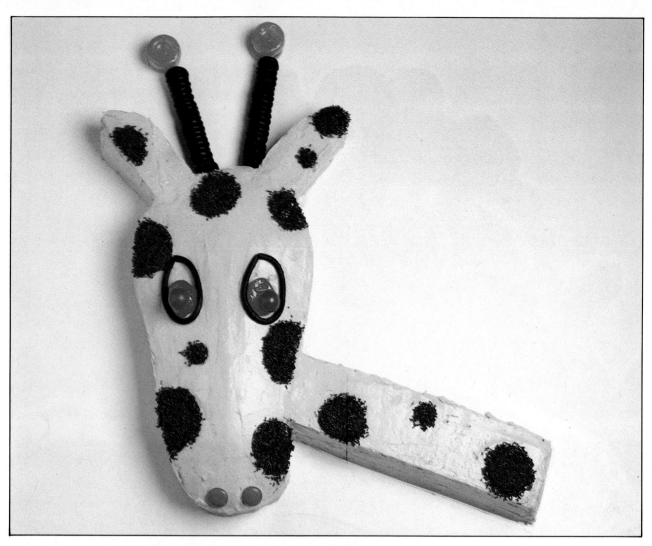

GEORGE GIRAFFE

2 packets butter cake mix
1 quantity Vienna Cream
yellow food colouring
chocolate sprinkles
licorice
assorted sweets (as shown)
2 candy sticks
1 board 45cm x 40cm (18in x 16in)

Make cakes according to directions on packet, pour half into greased 28cm x 18cm (11in x 7in) lamington tin, pour half of remaining mixture into greased 25cm x 8cm (10in x 3in) bar tin (you can make patty cakes with remaining mixture), bake both cakes in moderate oven 30 minutes or until cooked when tested. Turn on to wire rack to cool.

With a small sharp knife, cut out head and ears from lamington tin cake, as shown; cut bar tin cake in half horizontally, cut off one third, as shown, discard the small piece. Place large piece of bar tin cake on top of head; invert other section of bar tin cake, cut corner diagonally, as shown. Assemble giraffe, as shown, on prepared board.

Tint Vienna Cream with a few drops yellow food colouring, cover giraffe evenly with Vienna Cream; using different-sized scone cutters as guides, make spots with chocolate sprinkles. Eyes are outlined with licorice rounds, large round sweets with small round sweets in the centres represent eyes, two coloured sweets represent nostrils, candy sticks wound tightly with licorice represent horns. Place a large sweet at end of each horn, as shown.

LEONARD THE LION

3 packets butter cake mix
1½ quantities Vienna Cream
egg-yellow food colouring
30g (1oz) dark chocolate
2 white marshmallows
2 round flat green sweets
6 orange jubes
licorice
1 board 45cm x 35cm (18in x 14in)

Make cakes separately according to directions on packet, pour two quantities into two greased 28cm × 18cm (11in × 7in) lamington tins, pour the other quantity into greased 23cm × 12cm (9in × 5in) loaf tin, bake in moderate oven 30 minutes for lamington tins, 50 minutes for loaf tin or until cooked when tested. Stand 3 minutes, turn cakes on to wire racks to cool.

Trim top of loaf cake so it is flat, cut off one third of cake from one end (this small piece is not needed), split remaining two thirds in half horizontally, cut 4cm (1½in) piece from one end, as shown, for the nose, cut nose piece to a point. (Remaining piece

from which nose was cut is not needed.) Place lamington cakes side by side, trim sides where they join so they will fit closely together, trim tops if necessary so cakes are the same depth. Cut shape of lion's head, as shown. Assemble cake, as follows, on prepared board: place lamington cakes on board first, top with large oblong from loaf cake, position nose piece on top.

Tint Vienna Cream with egg-yellow food colouring, spread evenly over nose and face and around sides of cake. Spread cream thickly for mane, use a fork to give curly appearance. Melt chocolate over simmering water, dip fork in chocolate, shake off excess, use fork dipped in chocolate to define some of the curls, as shown; spread a little chocolate in triangular shape on end of nose. White marshmallows topped with small green sweets represent eyes, two cut orange jubes represent tongue, two orange jubes stacked one on top of the other represent each eyebrow, licorice strips represent whiskers.

PATTERNS FOR TIMOTHY TIGER

NOSE

HEAD (CUT TWO)

HOW TO CUT HEAD

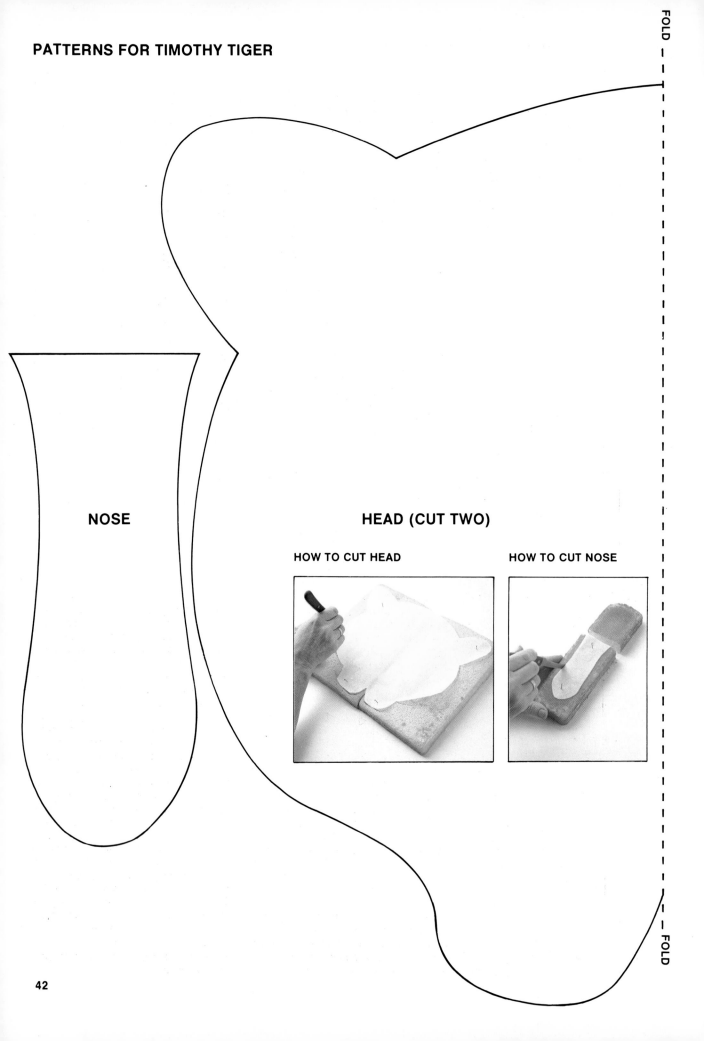

HOW TO CUT NOSE

TIMOTHY TIGER

2 packets butter cake mix
greaseproof paper
1½ quantities Vienna Cream
egg-yellow food colouring
2 white marshmallows
licorice
1 candied mint leaf
4 orange jubes

Make cakes together according to directions on packet, place 1½ cups of mixture into well-greased 25cm × 8cm (10in × 3in) bar tin, divide remaining mixture between two well-greased 28cm × 18cm (11in × 7in) lamington tins, bake in moderate oven 20 minutes for bar cake, 25 minutes for lamington cakes or until cooked when tested. Stand few minutes before turning on to wire racks to cool. Place large cakes side by side, trim off one long side of each cake so they sit flat against each other, trim tops, if necessary, to make sure they are the same height. Fold sheet of greaseproof paper in half, trace pattern for head, cut out with sharp scissors, unfold, pin on to lamington cakes, cut around pattern with sharp serrated knife. Trace pattern for nose on to greaseproof paper, cut out with sharp scissors, pin on to bar cake, cut around pattern with sharp serrated knife; cut nose at an angle, as shown, so it will sit almost flat on tiger's face near eyes. Position pieces of cake for face on prepared board, join with a little Vienna Cream.

Tint Vienna Cream with egg-yellow food colouring (you will need at least 1 teaspoon colouring to achieve a bright orange), spread cream over sides and top of face, position nose, cover with orange Vienna Cream. To make eyes, press marshmallows flat with fingers, position on cake, outline with licorice, cut mint leaf in half horizontally, trim to shape with scissors, place in position on marshmallow, top with small piece licorice to represent pupil. Cut two jubes for tongue, cut remaining two jubes for eyebrows, as shown, outline with licorice, as shown. For tiger's stripes, split tubular licorice with scissors, as shown (if possible, use pinking shears for an attractive finish), press licorice out flat, position stripes on face, as shown.

TEDDY BEAR

2 packets butter cake mix
wooden skewer
4 Chocolate Monte biscuits
1 quantity Fluffy Frosting (3 egg
  white quantity)
yellow food colouring
chocolate sprinkles
2 jubes
2 small sweets for pupils
1 round chocolate for nose
licorice
ribbon
1 board 63cm x 43cm (25in x 17in)

Make cakes according to directions on packet, pour just over half into greased deep 23cm (9in) round cake tin, pour remaining mixture into greased deep 20cm (8in) round cake tin (mixture should be same depth in both tins), bake in moderate oven 40 to 45 minutes or until cooked when tested. Turn on to wire rack to cool.

Cut out cakes, as shown; assemble bear, as shown, on prepared board (arms, body and one leg come from the larger cake, head and second leg come from the smaller). Use a small piece from head trimmings to extend the second leg, as shown; secure with small wooden skewer. With a sharp knife, shave paws and feet at a slight angle so that chocolate biscuits appear to be underneath. Tint frosting with yellow food colouring, spread all over bear, position chocolate biscuits, place 1 teaspoon chocolate sprinkles in each ear. Cut 1 jube in half, place a small coloured sweet in centre of each cut side, place in position for eyes, place a whole jube in centre of tummy. Round chocolate represents nose, thin strips licorice represent mouth. Tie ribbon in large bow, place under mouth.

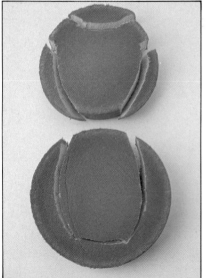

CUDDLY KOALA

2 packets butter cake mix
1 quantity chocolate Vienna Cream
1 tablespoon cocoa
2 tablespoons hot water
3 cups coconut
2 large sweets for eyes
2 small sweets for pupils
licorice
1 Chocolate Monte biscuit
candy mint leaves
1 board 60cm x 50cm (24in x 20in)

Make cakes according to directions on packet, divide between greased deep 23cm (9in) square cake tin and two deep 18cm (7in) round cake tins, or sandwich tins, so that mixture is same depth in each tin, bake in moderate oven 40 minutes for square tin, 30 minutes for round tins or until cooked when tested. Turn cakes on to wire racks to cool.

Leave one round cake whole for the head, cut other round cake in half horizontally; using a 12cm (5in) round cutter, cut each half into smaller rounds for ears. Cut square cake, as shown, to make body and paws. Assemble on a board, as shown, to form koala. Ice top and sides of cake with Vienna Cream. Mix together cocoa and hot water, add three quarters cocoa mixture to 2 cups coconut to tint it dark brown, add remaining quarter cocoa mixture to remaining cup coconut to tint it light brown; press light-coloured coconut on centre of ears, front of body, under arms and at tops of legs, as shown; press darker coconut over rest of body. Press on large round sweets then small round sweets to represent eyes; licorice cut to shape represents eyelashes and claws, chocolate biscuit represents nose. Arrange mint leaves around koala to represent tree, as shown.

CRAWLY CATERPILLAR
1 packet butter cake mix
1 quantity Vienna Cream
green food colouring
250g (8oz) shredded coconut
toothpicks
small piece coloured cardboard
1 pipecleaner
assorted sweets (as shown)

Make cake according to directions on packet, spoon tablespoonsful into deep greased patty tins (it makes about 24 cakes), bake in moderately hot oven 12 to 15 minutes or until golden brown. Cool on wire rack.

Tint Vienna Cream with green food colouring, press fork in sides of cakes, cover entire cakes with Vienna Cream, roll in green-tinted shredded coconut to coat completely. (Allowing one patty cake per guest, coat the number required.) Join cakes together with toothpicks to form caterpillar. Cut small piece coloured cardboard to fit head of caterpillar to represent "bonnet", press firmly into place, as shown. Pipecleaner represents feelers, assorted sweets, as shown, represent eyes, mouth and legs.

MILDRED MOUSE
1 packet butter cake mix
1 quantity Vienna Cream
coconut
licorice
pink marshmallows
white pipecleaners

Make cake according to directions on packet, pour into well-greased 1 litre (4 cup) pudding steamer, bake in moderate oven 60 minutes or until cooked when tested. Turn on to wire rack to cool.

Trim top of cake so mouse's body will sit flat, invert cake on prepared board, cut into mouse shape by sloping sides, trim to a slight point at one end to define nose, cut away all "browning" so finished mouse is as white as possible. Spread evenly with Vienna Cream, sprinkle thickly with coconut, press coconut on firmly. Twist licorice piece to represent tail, position at broad end of mouse; halved marshmallows represent ears and nose, small rounds of licorice represent eyes, white pipecleaners represent whiskers.

BEAUTIFUL BUTTERFLY

1 packet butter cake mix
1 quantity Vienna Cream
apricot food colouring
licorice
assorted sweets (as shown)

Make cake according to directions on packet, pour into greased deep 25cm (10in) round cake tin, bake in moderate oven 30 to 35 minutes or until cooked when tested. Turn on to wire rack to cool.

Cut and assemble cake, as shown, to form butterfly. Tint Vienna Cream with apricot food colouring, cover top and sides of cake with Vienna Cream. Licorice strips represent feelers and patterns on wings. Decorate with assorted sweets, as shown.

PINK ELEPHANT
2 packets butter cake mix
1½ quantities Vienna Cream
pink food colouring
250g (8oz) shredded coconut
round chocolate-coated biscuit
licorice
assorted sweets (as shown)
1 board 55cm x 35cm (22in x 14in)
Make cakes according to directions on packet, spoon evenly into two deep 20cm (8in) round cake tins, bake in moderate oven 50 minutes or until cooked when tested. Turn on to wire rack to cool.

Trim around edge of one cake to form elephant's body. Cut 11cm (4½in) circle from centre of other cake to form head, halve outside circle; one half is used for the trunk, wedges cut from other half form legs. Assemble cake, as shown, tint Vienna Cream with pink food colouring, ice elephant, cover with pink-tinted coconut. Chocolate biscuit represents ear, licorice strands represent tail. Use small sweets, as shown, for Pink Elephant's eye, tusk and toes.

JUNGLE ELEPHANT
2 packets butter cake mix
1 quantity Vienna Cream
pink food colouring
assorted sweets (as shown)
icecream wafer
licorice
coloured pipecleaners
1 board 50cm x 43cm (20in x 17in)

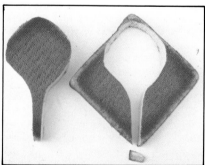

Make cakes according to directions on packet, pour half into greased 23cm (9in) square slab tin, divide remaining mixture between two greased 20cm (8in) sandwich tins, bake in moderate oven 35 minutes for large cake, 25 minutes for smaller cakes or until cooked when tested. Turn on to wire rack to cool. (Only one round cake is required for the elephant; the other can be frozen for later use.)

With a small sharp knife, cut large circle shape from one corner of square cake, gradually tapering circle to opposite corner to form elephant's head and trunk, trim cake at end of

trunk so it is even. Cut out ears from round cake, as shown. Assemble elephant, as shown, on prepared board, so that ears and head fit closely together.

Tint Vienna Cream with pink food colouring; reserve $\frac{1}{2}$ cup for inside of ears, tint remaining Vienna Cream with more pink food colouring so that it becomes a deeper shade. Cover elephant's head, trunk and outer ears with deep pink cream, cover insides of ears with lighter pink, arrange coloured sweets, as shown, to divide inner and outer ears. Cut icecream wafer, as shown, to represent tusks, make two slits in trunk, one on either side, insert tusks. Strips of licorice represent eyebrows and eyelashes, large round sweets with small coloured sweets in the centres represent eyes. Curl a few pipecleaners to represent hair.

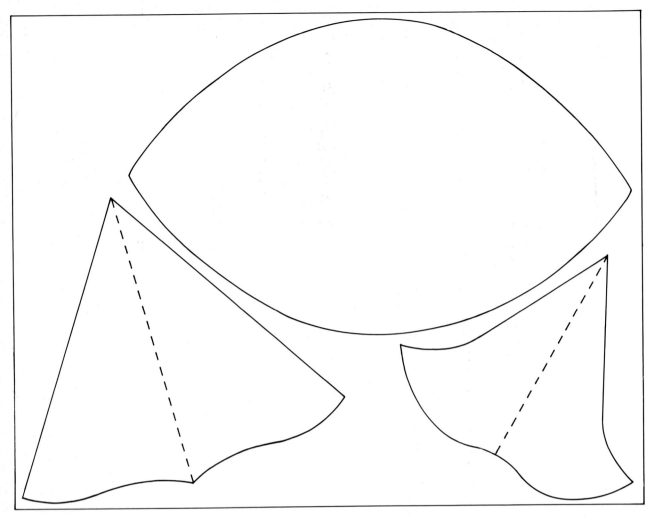

BUNNY RABBIT

2 packets butter cake mix
greaseproof paper
2 quantities Vienna Cream
pink food colouring
coconut
licorice
assorted sweets (as shown)
green food colouring
1 board 65cm x 40cm (26in x 16in)

Make cakes according to directions on packet, divide evenly between three deep 20cm (8in) round cake tins, bake in moderate oven 40 minutes or until cooked when tested. Turn on to wire racks to cool. Place three cakes side by side; trim, so they are all the same thickness.

Place sheet of greaseproof paper over patterns for feet and ears, trace them on to paper, cut out with sharp scissors; pin patterns on one cake, as shown. With sharp serrated knife, cut around pattern carefully, cut piece for back feet in two, as shown, cut pieces for front feet in two also. For front feet, take the two pieces of cake, cut diagonally from narrow end to broad end to taper (you only need two pieces for front feet, so discard other two pieces); cut 1cm (½in) from narrow ends of front feet.

Assemble bunny on board, as shown (picture shows final assembly but in fact feet and ears are iced before being positioned). Tint 1 tablespoon Vienna Cream with pink food colouring, cover cakes with remaining Vienna Cream, cover well with coconut. Cover feet with Vienna Cream, then coconut, place in position; thin strips licorice represent claws. Spread pink Vienna Cream in centres of ears, as shown, spread remaining area with plain Vienna Cream, cover well with coconut, place in position on head, sprinkle pink area with pink-tinted coconut. Coloured sweets represent eyes and nose, licorice pieces represent mouth and whiskers, green-tinted coconut around bunny's feet represents grass.

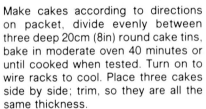

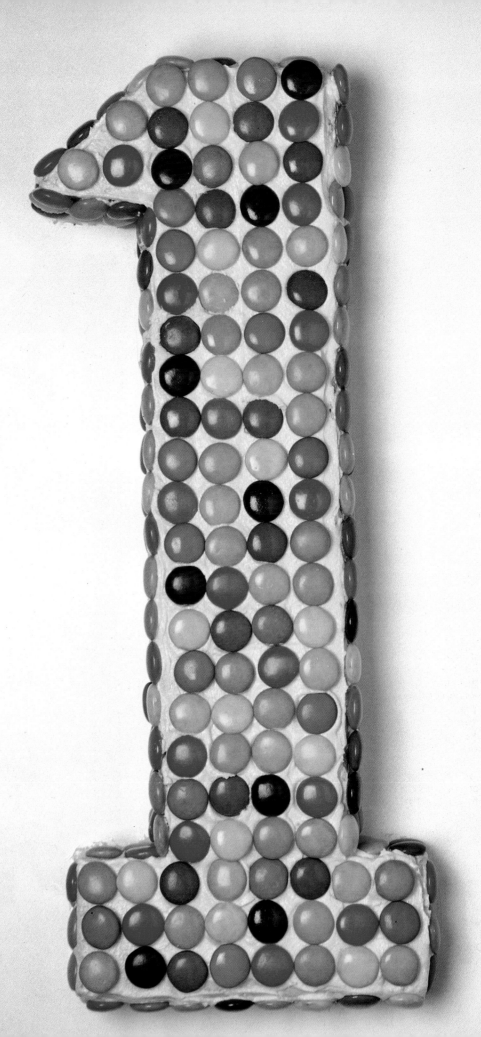

NUMBERS

NUMBER ONE

1 packet butter cake mix
1 quantity Vienna Cream
yellow food colouring
4 x 100g packets Smarties or other
   small round coloured sweets

Make cake according to directions on packet, pour into two greased 25cm x 8cm (10in x 3in) bar tins, bake in moderate oven 30 to 35 minutes or until cooked when tested. Turn on to wire racks to cool.

Leave one bar cake whole, cut the other into three pieces, as shown. Assemble cake, as shown, on prepared board to form a figure 1. Tint Vienna Cream with a few drops yellow food colouring; using a small spatula, cover entire cake with Vienna Cream, then cover top and sides with Smarties or other coloured sweets, as shown.

Note: One-year-olds may be too small to eat the coloured sweets but they will certainly love the cake.

NUMBER TWO

2 packets butter cake mix
250g (8oz) coloured cake
sprinkles (see note)
1 quantity Vienna Cream
1 board 43cm x 25cm (17in x 10in)

Make cakes according to directions on packet; they can be made together in large basin of electric mixer. Pour half into greased 28cm x 18cm (11in x 7in) lamington tin, pour the rest into two 25cm x 8cm (10in x 3in) bar tins (only one bar cake is needed; you can freeze the other for future use), bake in moderate oven 30 minutes or until cooked when tested. Turn on to wire rack to cool.

Trim tops of cakes to the same depth so they will sit flat. Place rectangular cake top side down on flat surface, place bar cake top side down at narrow end of rectangular cake, cut out a figure 2, as shown.

Cut jigsaw-shaped pieces from cake, as shown. Empty coloured sprinkles on to five individual pieces of paper, keeping colours separate. Work with one piece of jigsaw at a time; spread top, and sides which will show, with Vienna Cream, roll in one of the sprinkle colours, place in position on prepared board, spread a little more Vienna Cream on the side where next piece of jigsaw will fit. Continue until all pieces are coloured and fitted together.

Note: The coloured cake sprinkles are sold in individual packets or in 125g packets containing five colours under the name Dollar Fives; you will need two packets.

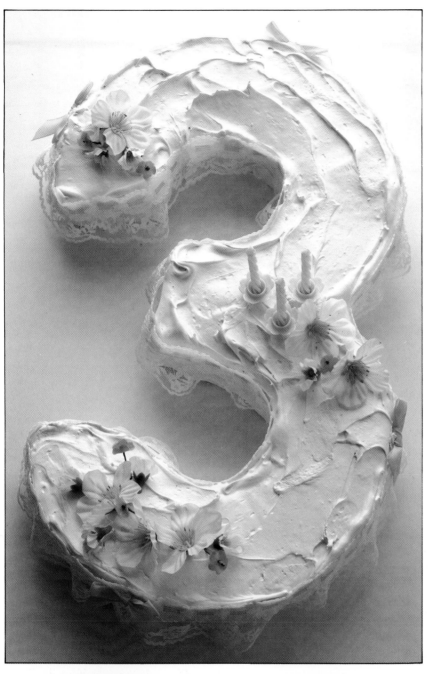

NUMBER THREE

2 packets butter cake mix
1 quantity Fluffy Frosting (2 egg
   white quantity)
pink food colouring
2 metres nylon lace
½ metre nylon ribbon
artificial flowers
candles

Make cakes according to directions on packet, divide evenly and pour into two greased 20cm (8in) ring tins, bake in moderate oven 35 to 40 minutes or until cooked when tested. Turn on to wire racks to cool. Cut out pieces and join cakes together, as shown, on prepared board.

Tint frosting with food colouring, spread over top and sides of cake. Press lace around outside edge, make small bows from nylon ribbon; use a little leftover frosting to stick bows to side of cake. Decorate top with flowers and candles.

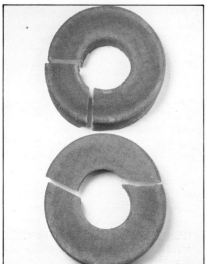

55

NUMBER FOUR

1 packet butter cake mix
1 quantity Vienna Cream
red food colouring
marshmallow flowers (see page 4)
round pink sweets
hundreds and thousands

Make cake according to directions on packet, pour into greased 28cm x 18cm (11in x 7in) lamington tin, bake in moderate oven 30 minutes or until cooked when tested. Turn on to wire rack to cool.

Cut cake vertically into three, as shown. Leave one piece whole, cut remaining two into three sections each, as shown. Assemble pieces on prepared board to make a figure 4 (the three remaining pieces are not required). Tint Vienna Cream with a few drops red food colouring to a deep pink. Ice top and sides of cake with Vienna Cream.

Make marshmallow flowers (see page 4), place a round pink sweet in centre of each, sprinkle half the flowers with hundreds and thousands, leave other half plain, arrange flowers on cake, as shown.

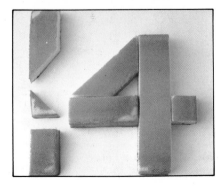

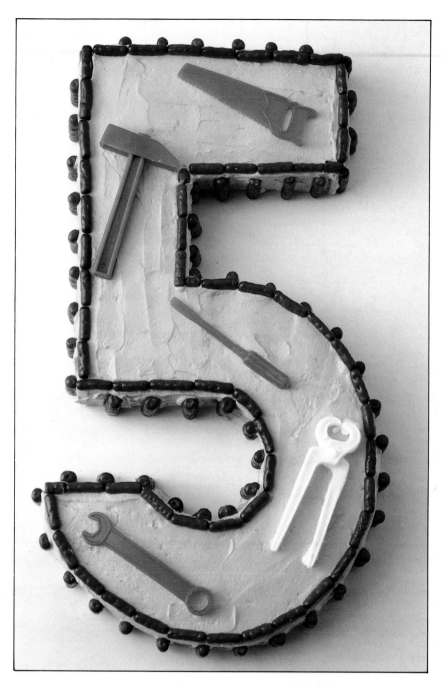

NUMBER FIVE

1 packet butter cake mix
1 quantity Vienna Cream
yellow food colouring
licorice "bullets"
toy plastic tool set

Make cake according to directions on packet, divide between well-greased 25cm x 8cm (10in x 3in) bar tin and 20cm (8in) ring tin so that both are about the same depth, bake in moderate oven 30 to 35 minutes or until cooked when tested. Turn on to wire racks to cool.

Cut bar cake in half horizontally; cut ring, as shown (the three smaller pieces are not required). Assemble the remaining pieces on prepared board to form a figure 5, as shown. Colour Vienna Cream with a few drops yellow food colouring, ice cake top and sides. Decorate sides and top edge with licorice "bullets", arrange tools on top, as shown.

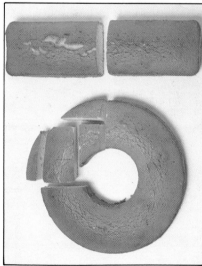

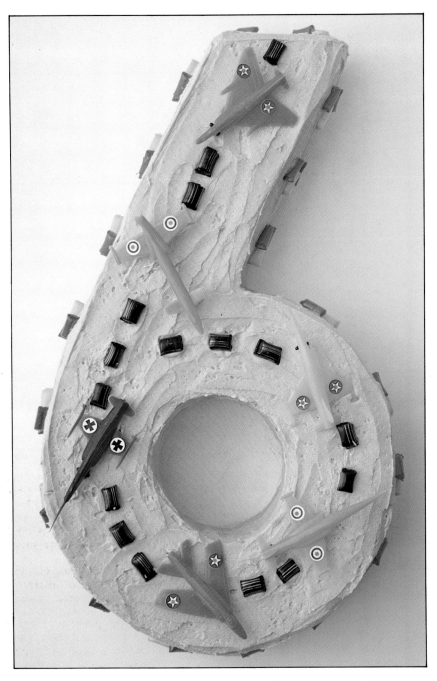

NUMBER SIX
1 packet butter cake mix
1 quantity Vienna Cream
green food colouring
red, yellow and black sweets
6 plastic aeroplanes

Make cake according to directions on packet, divide between greased 25cm x 8cm (10in x 3in) bar tin and 20cm (8in) ring tin so that both mixtures are the same depth, bake in moderate oven 30 to 35 minutes or until cooked when tested. Turn on to wire rack to cool.

Leave ring cake whole; cut bar cake, as shown. Assemble cake, as shown, on prepared board to make a figure 6. Tint Vienna Cream with a few drops green food colouring, ice cake. Decorate sides with red and yellow sweets to form arrows, decorate top with black sweets to form runway; place planes, as shown.

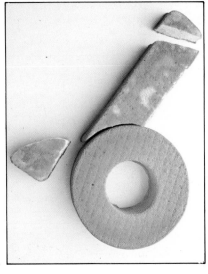

NUMBER SEVEN
1 packet butter cake mix
1 quantity Vienna Cream
purple food colouring
3 packets pink Lifesavers
4 packets white Lifesavers
small pink musks

Make cake according to directions on packet, divide evenly and pour into two greased 25cm x 8cm (10in x 3in) bar tins, bake in moderate oven 30 to 35 minutes or until cooked when tested. Turn on to wire racks to cool.

Leave one cake whole, cut the other into two, as shown. Assemble cake, as shown, on prepared board to make a figure 7. Tint Vienna Cream with a few drops food colouring, cover top and sides of entire cake with Vienna Cream, decorate with halved Lifesavers and small musks, as shown.

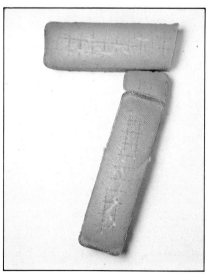

NUMBER EIGHT
2 packets butter cake mix
1 quantity Fluffy Frosting
(2 egg white quantity)
yellow food colouring
green-tinted coconut
8 plastic moonmen toys
silver cachous
small sweets (as shown)

Make cakes according to directions on packet, divide between greased 20cm (8in) ring tin and 15cm (6in) ring tin so that both mixtures are the same depth, halfway up sides of tins (any leftover mixture can be used for patty cakes), bake in moderate oven 30 minutes for 15cm (6in), 35 minutes for 20cm (8in) cake or until cooked when tested. Turn on to wire rack to cool.

Trim cakes, if necessary, so they are equal in height and will lie flat. Cut cakes, as shown; assemble on board to make a figure 8. Tint Fluffy Frosting with a few drops yellow food colouring, cover sides of cake with frosting, cover top roughly to represent moon surface, cover sides with green coconut. Arrange moonmen, and decorate with cachous and sweets, as shown.

Note: If 15cm (6in) ring tin is not available, a 20cm (8in) ring tin can be used and cake cut down to the size of a 15cm (6in) ring. If using two 20cm (8in) ring tins, you will need all the cake mixture.

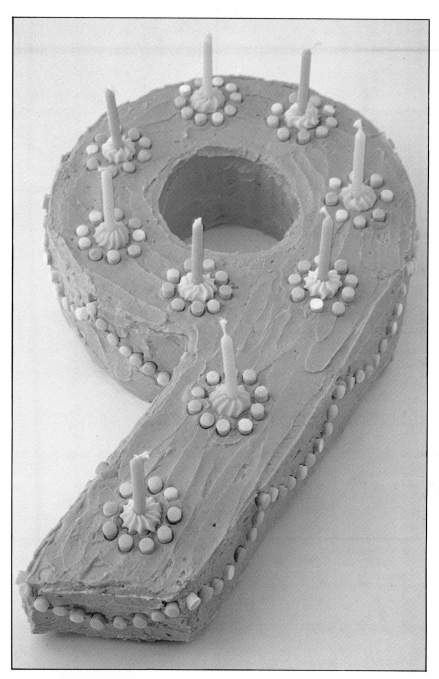

NUMBER NINE
1 packet butter cake mix
1 quantity Vienna Cream
green food colouring
small round sweets
9 candles

Make cake according to directions on packet, divide between greased 25cm x 8cm (10in x 3in) bar tin and 20cm (8in) ring tin so that both mixtures are the same depth, bake in moderate oven 30 to 35 minutes or until cooked when tested. Turn on to wire rack to cool.

Leave ring cake whole; cut bar cake, as shown. Assemble, as shown, on prepared board to make a figure 9. Tint Vienna Cream with few drops green food colouring; spread over cake. Decorate sides with sweets in a scallop pattern; make flower designs with sweets and candles, as shown.

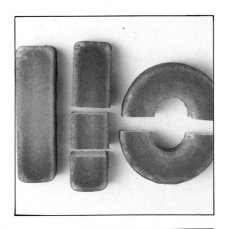

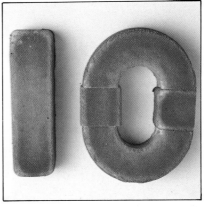

NUMBER TEN
2 packets butter cake mix
2 cups coconut
300ml carton cream
30g (1oz) dark chocolate
CHOCOLATE ICING
3 cups icing sugar
½ cup cocoa
1 cup warm water
3 tablespoons apricot jam

Cake: Make cakes according to directions on packet, divide between greased 20cm (8in) ring tin and two greased 25cm x 8cm (10in x 3in) bar tins so that all mixtures are the same depth, bake in moderate oven 30 minutes for bar tins, 40 minutes for ring or until cooked when tested. Turn on to wire racks to cool. Leave one bar cake whole; cut the other into three pieces, as shown. Cut ring in half, as shown. Arrange pieces on prepared board, as shown.

Chocolate Icing: Combine sifted icing sugar and sifted cocoa, mix well. Gradually add combined water and apricot jam, stirring until all liquid has been added and mixture is smooth; push through wire sieve.

Pour the chocolate icing into a large baking dish or other flat dish; sprinkle coconut on a large sheet of greaseproof paper. Taking one piece of cake at a time, dip into chocolate icing until evenly coated all round, lift from mixture, hold above dish for 1 minute to allow excess icing to drain off. Place iced cake in coconut, toss gently until completely coated, remove, place on greaseproof paper 10 minutes to allow icing to dry. Repeat with remaining four pieces. Reassemble iced pieces on prepared board to make number 10. Beat cream until soft peaks form, pipe decoratively around centres of cakes, as shown; sprinkle top with grated chocolate.

ICECREAM CAKES

HEART

2 litre carton icecream
aluminium foil
2 x 300ml cartons
**   thickened cream**
¾ cup icing sugar
pink food colouring

Place softened icecream in bowl, use potato masher to break down icecream until just beginning to melt, pour into deep 18cm (7in) heart shaped tin, cover with aluminium foil, freeze overnight. Run a spatula or knife around inside edge of tin, invert tin on to serving plate, run hot cloth over base of tin, lift off tin. Return cake to freezer, freeze overnight.

Divide cream evenly into three separate bowls, add ¼ cup sifted icing sugar to each; whip cream until firm peaks form, tint each lot with different quantities of pink food colouring, ranging from light pink through medium pink to deep pink. You will need three piping bags fitted with star tubes. Fill each bag with a different shade of pink cream, pipe around sides and top of cake, as shown. If icecream begins to melt, return to freezer until it firms. When piping is completed, freeze cake several hours.
Note: If you do not have three piping bags, wash out one bag and tube after each use and dry thoroughly. While bag is being washed and dried, return icecream cake to freezer.

SHIP

**2 empty cardboard boxes (from foil,
  plastic food wrap or waxed paper)
aluminium foil
2 litre carton vanilla icecream
red food colouring
purple food colouring
assorted sweets (as shown)
85g packet lime jelly crystals
licorice**

Separate lids from boxes, undo one end of one box, clip or staple two side pieces together to join at a point at the folds to form mould for body of ship. Line both boxes with aluminium foil.

Place half softened icecream and a few drops red food colouring in bowl, use potato masher to break down icecream until just beginning to melt and colour is even, spoon mixture into mould for body of ship, smooth top, cover with aluminium foil, freeze overnight or until firm.

Tint two thirds remaining icecream with a few drops purple food colouring, break down with masher, as above, spoon mixture into other box to two thirds of its length, fill remaining space with rest of untinted icecream, smooth top, cover with aluminium foil, freeze overnight or until firm. Loosen edges, turn body of ship out from

mould on to long chilled plate, return to freezer, freeze until firm. Turn other icecream out from mould on to a chilled tray, cut icecream in two where colours meet. Cut two 2.5cm (1in) rounds from one end of plain icecream, cut away a 2.5cm (1in) slice from side of remaining piece, straighten edges, round off corners at one end with a small knife. Cut away a 1cm (½in) slice from side of purple icecream, round off corners at one end. Return all pieces to freezer, freeze until firm.

Place white icecream on top of purple icecream then, with a long knife, slide the two layers on top of body of ship. Place one of the two cut-out rounds on top of ship, the other at back, as shown. Return cake to freezer, freeze until firm. Decorate with assorted sweets, as shown, by pressing sweets firmly into cake; return cake to freezer, freeze until firm. Make up jelly as directed on packet; when set, chop up. Just before serving, spoon jelly around ship, add anchor of licorice.

HAPPY BIRTHDAY ICECREAM CAKE

3 x 1 litre cartons icecream
yellow food colouring
aluminium foil
2 x 300ml cartons thickened cream
green food colouring
¾ cup icing sugar
apricot food colouring
orange food colouring

Place softened icecream and a few drops yellow food colouring in bowl, use potato masher to break down icecream until just beginning to melt and colour is even, pour into deep 23cm (9in) round cake tin, cover with aluminium foil, freeze overnight. Run a spatula or knife around inside edge of tin, invert tin on to serving plate, run hot cloth over base of tin, carefully lift off tin. Return cake to freezer, again freeze overnight.

Place ¼ cup cream in small bowl, tint with a few drops green food colouring, whip until soft peaks form. Divide remaining cream into three separate bowls, add ¼ cup sifted icing sugar to each; tint one lot yellow, one apricot and one orange. Whip each bowl of cream until soft peaks form; refrigerate until ready to use. Cover top of cake evenly with yellow cream.

Fill three piping bags fitted with star tubes each with a different coloured cream, pipe decorative border around cake, as shown, pipe to cover sides of cake, alternating rows of colour. Return cake to freezer for a few hours until icecream firms. Pipe star-shaped flowers, as shown, with remaining apricot cream and some of remaining orange cream.

Place green-tinted cream in small cone made of greaseproof paper (see page 4), cut small hole in end of cone, pipe stems on to flowers with green cream, pipe small leaves on to stems. Place remaining orange-tinted cream in small cone made of greaseproof paper, cut small hole in end of cone, pipe greeting across top of cake. Return to freezer. Remove from freezer 5 minutes before serving to thaw slightly and allow for easy cutting.

Note: If you do not have three piping bags, wash out one bag and tube after each use and dry thoroughly. While bag is being washed and dried, return icecream cake to freezer. For information on piping kits, see page 3.

BOOK

2 litre carton chocolate icecream
1 litre carton vanilla icecream
aluminium foil
1 birthday card
toothpicks or round-headed pins
300ml carton cream

Remove icecream from freezer 10 minutes before using, so it will be easier to handle; do not allow to melt. Line 28cm × 18cm (11in × 7in) lamington tin with aluminium foil, bringing foil up and over long sides of tin for easy removal of set icecream. Spread just under half the chocolate icecream over base of tin, making sure top and sides are even. Place in freezer, freeze until firm. When firm, spread enough chocolate icecream down one long side of tin to within 1cm (½in) of top of tin to make a 2.5cm (1in) border; this forms the spine of the book. Return to freezer, freeze until firm. When firm, spread vanilla icecream over top of chocolate icecream to level of chocolate icecream border; the vanilla icecream represents the pages of the book. Return to freezer, freeze until firm. When firm, spread remaining chocolate icecream completely over top, make smooth. Return to freezer, freeze until firm.

Remove from freezer, allow to stand 3 minutes, run a spatula or knife down unlined sides of tin, turn out icecream on to chilled serving plate. Decorate with picture cut from a birthday card, secure with toothpicks or round-headed pins. Whip cream until firm peaks form, place cream in piping bag fitted with a small star tube, pipe cream decoratively around edge of picture, as shown, around sides of book and down back of spine. Run a knife several times around white section to define leaves of book. Using a plain tube, pipe ''Happy Birthday'' above picture. During decoration, return cake to freezer at 5 minute intervals to keep it from thawing. Remove picture and toothpicks or pins before cutting.

Quick Draw McGraw Copyright © Hanna-Barbera Productions Inc.

DOLLY VARDEN

2 litre carton vanilla icecream
aluminium foil
1 small doll
2 x 300ml cartons thickened cream
¾ cup icing sugar
purple food colouring
gold cachous
coloured stars
1 coloured pipecleaner

Place softened icecream in bowl, use potato masher to break down icecream until just beginning to melt, pack into Dolly Varden tin, cover with aluminium foil, freeze overnight. Run spatula around inside edge of tin, invert on to serving plate, run hot cloth over base and sides, lift off tin. (If icecream remains in tin, dip base in hot water for a few seconds.) Return cake to freezer, freeze until firm.

With very sharp scissors or a sharp knife, cut doll at waist level; remove icecream from freezer, firmly position

doll in centre of icecream, as shown, freeze again until very firm. With a sharp knife, mark pattern on doll's skirt as guide for piping. Place ¾ cup cream and ¼ cup sifted icing sugar into each of three separate bowls. With food colouring, tint one lot of cream deep mauve, tint another paler mauve; leave the third lot plain. Whip each bowl of cream until firm peaks form. For decorating, you will need three piping bags fitted with star tubes. Fill each bag with a different-coloured cream, pipe alternate triangles of deep mauve, plain and paler mauve, as shown. If icecream begins to melt during piping, return to freezer until icecream and cream firm.

Smooth deep mauve cream over body of doll for bodice of dress, arrange gold cachous on top of bodice to represent neckline, arrange more gold cachous in a triangle from waist, decorate neck with coloured stars to

represent necklace; gold stars stuck to ears with a little Vienna Cream represent earrings, small piece coloured pipecleaner with gold cachou stuck on represents bracelet. Return cake to freezer until firm.

Note: If you do not have three piping bags, wash out one bag and tube after each use and dry thoroughly. While bag is being washed and dried, return icecream cake to freezer.

FRIENDLY FOLK

HAPPY CLOWN

1 packet butter cake mix
1 quantity Vienna Cream
2 teaspoons cocoa
2 icecream wafers
licorice allsorts
1 icecream cone
2 small flat lollipops
licorice
1 paper streamer
1 party hat
hundreds and thousands

Make cake according to directions on packet, pour into greased deep 20cm (8in) round cake tin, bake in moderate oven 50 minutes or until cooked when tested. Turn cake on to wire rack to cool.

Cut out shape of cheeks on either side, as shown. Tint 2 tablespoons Vienna Cream with sifted cocoa, spread over top of cake, as shown, to make hairline; spread plain Vienna Cream over rest of top and sides of cake. Wafers cut to shape, as shown, topped with licorice allsorts, represent eyes. Cut point off icecream cone, press point into cake to represent nose. Curve lollipop sticks into mouth shape, press on to cake. Licorice strips represent eyebrows, paper streamer represents hair; top with party hat. Cover tops and sides of trimmings with rest of plain Vienna Cream, coat with hundreds and thousands, press against base of cake to make bow tie.

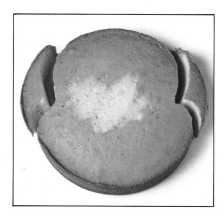

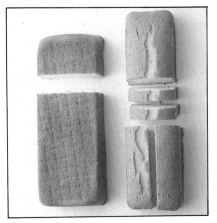

ROBERT ROBOT

1 packet butter cake mix
1 quantity Vienna Cream
blue food colouring
assorted sweets (as shown)
hundreds and thousands
2 pipe cleaners

Make cake according to directions on packet, divide mixture evenly into greased 25cm x 8cm (10in x 3in) bar tin and 20cm x 10cm (8in x 4in) loaf tin. Bake in moderate oven 30 minutes for bar tin and 35 to 40 minutes for loaf tin. Turn cakes on to wire rack to cool.

Slice top off loaf cake to make it level. Cut 5cm (2in) slice off one end of loaf cake, place slice, bottom side up, on one end of loaf cake to form shoulders. Cut 10cm (4in) slice off one end of bar cake. This forms the head. Cut two 1cm (½in) slices off the other piece of bar cake — these form the arms. Cut remaining piece of bar cake in half vertically, to form the feet. Assemble cake as shown. Colour Vienna Cream with a few drops of food colouring. Join head and shoulders to body with Vienna Cream, coat arms and feet with Vienna Cream, then roll in hundreds and thousands. Cover cake with Vienna Cream, place arms and feet into position. Decorate with assorted sweets; curl 2 pipe cleaners around pencil, remove pencil, insert pipe cleaners in head to represent antennae.

Note: If necessary, insert a long wooden skewer through head, shoulders and body to make cake stand more securely.

oven 1 hour for large cake, 45 minutes for smaller cake or until cooked when tested. Turn on to wire racks to cool. (Make patty cakes with any leftover mixture.)

Trim tops of cakes so they will sit flat, invert on to prepared board; cut chunky trimmings to make ears. Tint half Vienna Cream with 2 tablespoons sifted cocoa, cover large cake with brown Vienna Cream, leaving 1cm (½in) border around top to keep ruffle clean; do not ice top of cake. Decorate with round sweets and silver cachous, as shown.

Fold two lengths crepe paper as if to make a fan, join edges with sticky tape, fasten centre with paper clip, place on top of cake. Secure ears with a little plain Vienna Cream on either side of small cake, cover cake with Vienna Cream, place on top of ruffle. Tint shredded coconut with a few drops orange food colouring, sprinkle over ears. Decorate face and make hair, as shown, with thin licorice strips, glace cherries and sweets; top with party hat, as shown.

CLARENCE CLOWN
2 packets butter cake mix
2 quantities Vienna Cream
2 tablespoons cocoa
assorted sweets (as shown)
silver cachous
crepe paper
sticky tape
1 paper clip
shredded coconut
orange food colouring
licorice
glace cherries
1 party hat

Make cakes according to directions on packet, pour just over half into greased 1.25 litre (5 cup) pudding basin to three quarters fill it, pour half remaining mixture into greased 750ml (3 cup) pudding basin to three quarters fill it, bake in moderately slow

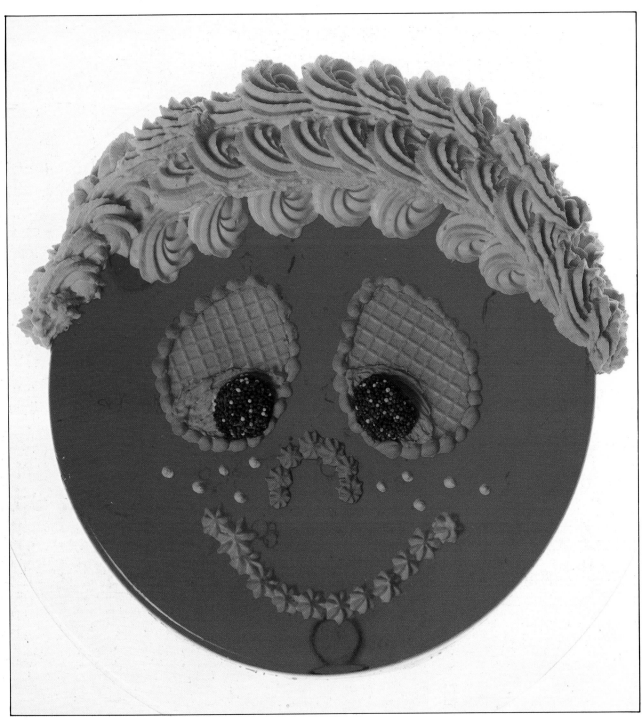

JOLLY JELLY CAKE
2 x 100g packets lime green
    jelly crystals
2 x 100g packets yellow
    jelly crystals
2 x 100g packets red jelly crystals
1½ litres (6 cups) hot water
300ml carton thickened cream
yellow food colouring
red food colouring
green food colouring
orange food colouring
2 pink icecream wafers
2 purple sweets

Make up green, yellow and red jellies in separate bowls using 2 cups hot water for each. Pour red jelly into deep 20cm (8in) round cake tin, refrigerate until set; pour cool yellow jelly over red jelly, refrigerate until set; pour cool green jelly over yellow jelly, refrigerate until set. To turn out cake, wipe underside of tin with very hot cloth, invert on to serving dish.

Tint half the cream with yellow food colouring; divide other half into three equal portions, tint one portion pink with red food colouring, one with green food colouring and one with orange food colouring. Beat all portions of cream until soft peaks form. Cut icecream wafers into pear shapes; position, as shown, to represent eyes. Using piping bag and small plain pipe, pipe around edges of wafers and in corners with pink Vienna Cream, as shown; position sweets, as shown, to represent eyeballs. Using piping bag and shell tube, pipe yellow Vienna Cream over top and sides of cake, as shown, to represent hair. Using piping bag and small star pipe, pipe a nose with green Vienna Cream; with the same pipe, pipe a mouth with orange Vienna Cream. Using a small plain pipe, pipe dots of yellow Vienna Cream.
Note: For information on small piping sets, see page 4.

MISTER MONSTER
1 packet butter cake mix
1 quantity chocolate Vienna Cream
licorice
musk sticks
hundreds and thousands
assorted sweets (as shown)

Make cake according to directions on packet, pour into greased 28cm × 18cm (11in × 7in) lamington tin, bake in moderate oven 30 minutes or until cooked when tested. Turn on to wire rack to cool. Cover top and sides of cake evenly with Vienna Cream, decorate with licorice, musk sticks, hundreds and thousands and assorted sweets, as shown. We used Kool Mints and Smarties for eyes; oblong marshmallows cut to a pointed shape represent the teeth.

FRIENDLY GHOST
1 packet butter cake mix
1 quantity Fluffy Frosting
  (3 egg white quantity)
2 eggshells
assorted sweets (as shown)
pink food colouring
coconut

Make cake according to directions on packet, pour into greased 28cm × 18cm (11in × 7in) lamington tin, bake in moderate oven 30 minutes or until cooked when tested. Turn on to wire rack to cool.

Cut out cake, as shown, place on board, position cut-off corners halfway down sides of cake to represent up-held arms, as shown. Cover cake with Fluffy Frosting, make small peaks on top of head to represent hair. Position halved cleaned eggshells to represent eyes, place round sweet in centre of each; string of small sweets represents mouth. Surround cake with pink-tinted coconut.

THE GOOD WITCH

1 packet butter cake mix
1 quantity Vienna Cream
blue food colouring
purple food colouring
thin licorice
2 round sweets for eyes
1 small packet potato straws
1 piece thick licorice

Make cake according to directions on packet, pour into greased 28cm × 18cm (11in × 7in) lamington tin, bake in moderate oven 30 minutes or until cooked when tested. Turn on to wire rack to cool.

Cut cake, as shown, assemble on prepared board. Tint ½ cup Vienna Cream with a few drops blue food colouring, tint remaining Vienna Cream with purple food colouring, cover face and hands with blue Vienna Cream, cover top and sides of rest of cake with purple Vienna Cream. remove fondant pieces from licorice allsorts, as shown, cut out stars with small sharp-pointed knife, position on witch's dress, as shown. Decorate with thin licorice and assorted sweets, as shown; potato straws represent hair. To assemble broom, cut piece thick licorice in half, position one half near hand, position other half at bottom of cake, as shown. Thin licorice represents bristles; wind piece thin licorice around joint.

FOR BOYS

ROCKET

3 packets butter cake mix
heavy cardboard
aluminium foil
11cm (4½in) flan tin
wooden toothpicks
2 quantities Vienna Cream
apricot food colouring
candy sticks
assorted sweets (as shown)
coloured paper
birthday candles

Make cake according to directions on packet, three quarters fill greased 2 cup pudding basin, pour rest of mixture into greased deep 25cm (10in) square tin, bake in moderate oven 25 to 30 minutes for pudding basin cake, 1¼ hours for square cake or until cooked when tested. Turn on to wire racks to cool.

Following pattern (see overleaf), cut rocket fins from cardboard, cover neatly with aluminium foil. Assemble fins by sliding slits together in centre; secure by placing flan tin upside down in centre to hold fins firmly and form base of rocket.

Cut square cake in half vertically, stand two halves upright with bases together, as shown, place pudding basin cake on top, secure with wooden toothpicks. Trim corners to form a cylindrical shape, as shown, using pudding basin cake on top as guide; position rocket on flan tin, as shown. Tint Vienna Cream with apricot food colouring, spread Vienna Cream over entire cake. Decorate with candy sticks and assorted sweets, as shown. Make cone from coloured paper, place on top of cake to represent nose cone of rocket, position candles around base of nose cone, as shown.

Turn to next page for fins pattern.

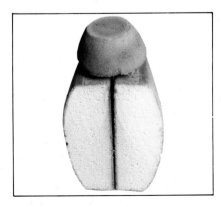

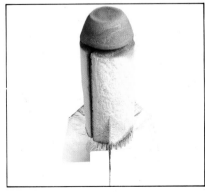

PATTERN FOR ROCKET FINS (CUT TWO)

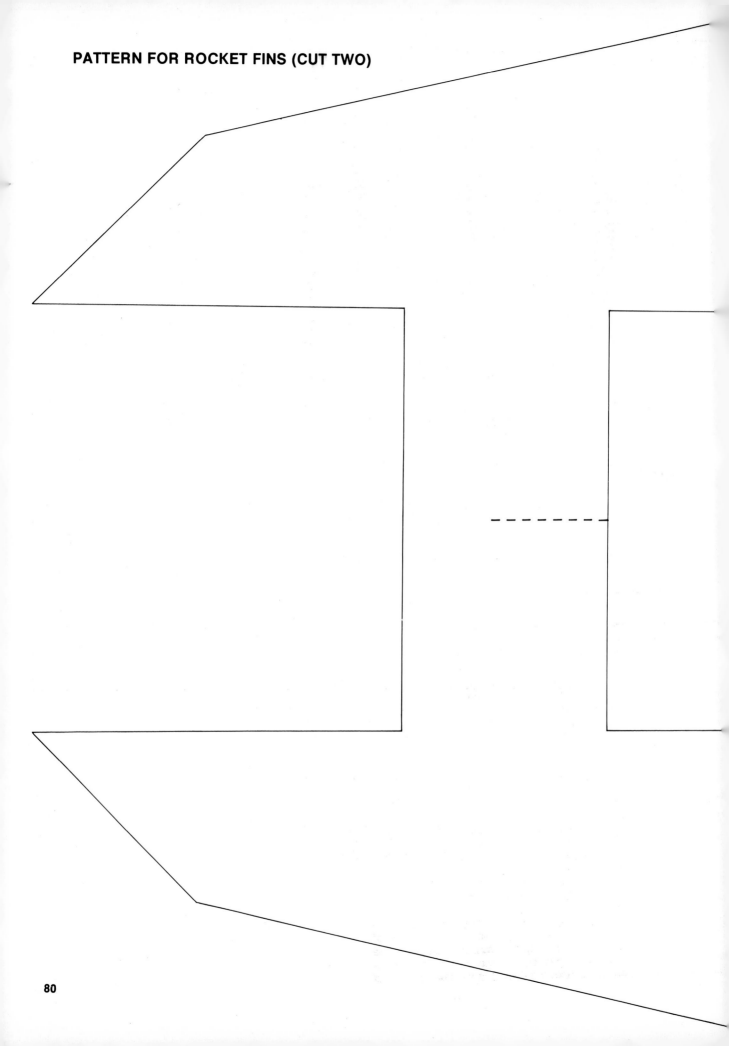

PIRATE

1 packet butter cake mix
1 quantity Vienna Cream
apricot food colouring
1 icecream wafer
assorted sweets (as shown)
1 round chocolate biscuit
licorice

Make cake according to directions on packet, pour into greased deep 23cm (9in) round cake tin, bake in moderate oven 45 minutes or until cooked when tested. Turn on to wire rack to cool.

Trim top of cake to shape of pirate's hat, as shown; tint one quarter Vienna Cream with apricot food colouring, spread carefully over hat, as shown. Spread remaining Vienna Cream over rest of cake for pirate's face, shape icecream wafer for pirate's ear, cover with Vienna Cream, press ear into side of cake; chocolate coin (or ring jube) represents earring. Make small skull and crossbones out of paper, place on pirate's hat. Trim one side of chocolate biscuit, position on face to represent eye patch, as shown; licorice represents strap of patch. We used red jelly snake for mouth, chocolate "bullets" and jelly bean for eye, licorice for moustache, chocolate "clinker" for nose, trimmed coloured musk sticks for hair.

SPORTS CAR
1 packet butter cake mix
1 quantity Vienna Cream
green food colouring
¾ cup coconut
licorice
2 green musk sticks
assorted sweets (as shown)
1 pipecleaner

Make cake according to directions on packet, pour into greased 20cm x 10cm (8in x 4in) loaf tin, bake in moderate oven 50 minutes or until cooked when tested. Turn cake on to wire rack to cool.

With a serrated knife, slice off one end at a sharp angle to about 2.5cm (1in) from base for back of car, slice other end at a less acute angle for front of car; place on prepared board. Tint Vienna Cream with a few drops green food colouring; tint coconut green too. Cut off a small chunk from each piece of cake trimmings, place under cake where front and back wheels will go.

Cover top and sides with Vienna Cream, sprinkle coconut on roof, along sides and centre of bonnet, as shown, for a sporty effect. Thin strips licorice represent windows, musk stick strips give lines to the car, small sweets represent rear vision mirror, headlights, door handles and the numberplate, licorice scraps make steering wheel and bumper bars, pipecleaner represents radio aerial.

RACING CAR

1 packet butter cake mix
1 quantity Vienna Cream
apricot food colouring
assorted sweets (as shown)
licorice
chocolate sprinkles

Make cake according to directions on packet, pour into greased 28cm x 18cm (11in x 7in) lamington tin, bake in moderate oven 30 to 35 minutes or until cooked when tested. Turn on to wire rack to cool.

With a 5cm (2in) plain cutter, cut four rounds from along one long side for wheels; from top corner of opposite side, cut a slice 2.5cm x 10cm (1in x 4in), then cut the slice diagonally in two from corner to corner to make two triangular pieces. Cut a 1cm (½in) slice from along rest of side to form base support for body of car. Assemble cake on prepared board. Trim ends of main cake, as shown; gently scoop out semicircle two thirds down from front of car for seat, place one triangular piece on either side of semicircle, as shown; position car over base support. Tint Vienna Cream with a few drops food colouring, cover top and sides of car with Vienna Cream, decorate with assorted sweets, as shown; jube ring wrapped around thick licorice piece represents steering wheel. Cover wheels with Vienna Cream, roll in chocolate sprinkles to coat completely, place round sweets in centres, position wheels on car.

WIGWAM
2 packets butter cake mix
coloured foil
1 quantity Vienna Cream
assorted sweets (as shown)
wooden skewers
1 packet toy cowboys and Indians

Make cakes according to directions on packet, pour three quarters into well-greased Dolly Varden tin, spoon remaining mixture into 12 greased patty pans, bake patty cakes in moderate oven 15 to 20 minutes or until cooked when tested. Remove from oven. Reduce heat to moderately slow, cook large cake 1¼ hours or until cooked when tested. Cool in tin 10 minutes, turn on to wire rack.

When cold, trim top evenly with serrated knife, place cake, broad end down, on board covered with coloured foil, cover cake with Vienna Cream, decorate with sweets, as shown, press wooden skewers into top, position cowboys and Indians on board. Ice patty cakes and serve separately.

Note: Dolly Varden tins are available in kitchenware departments of most large stores; if you have trouble finding one, see note on page 5. Packets of cowboys and Indians are obtainable at variety stores, toy shops and toy departments of most large stores.

HELICOPTER

1 packet butter cake mix
1 quantity Vienna Cream
apricot food colouring
blue food colouring
assorted sweets (as shown)
5 icecream wafers
3 pipecleaners
coconut
green food colouring

Make cake according to directions on packet, pour into greased 28cm x 18cm (11in x 7in) lamington tin, bake in moderate oven 30 minutes or until cooked when tested. Turn on to wire rack to cool. Cut cake, as shown; remove large central piece and two semicircles at sides. Cut two strips between large central piece and semicircles at sides in two horizontally, giving one wide and one narrow piece from each strip; round off ends of wide pieces to resemble skis. Place two semicircular pieces together to form circle, position circle on top of main body piece, as shown, trim edges of both to dome shape, as shown. Tint ½ cup Vienna Cream with a few drops apricot food colouring, spread over tops and sides of "skis", position "skis" on prepared board, place body of helicopter over "skis". Tint remaining Vienna Cream with blue food colouring, spread over top and sides of body of helicopter. Decorate with assorted sweets, as shown.

Cut one icecream wafer into propeller shape, press into position at rear of helicopter. Make a cross with two pipecleaners, secure in centre with third pipecleaner, then fold this in half, twist to form stem, push through centre of dome. Trim remaining four icecream wafers to shape, as shown, stick on to pipecleaners with apricot Vienna Cream. Tint coconut with green food colouring, sprinkle around helicopter; place small white sweets in circle around cake, as shown, to represent helicopter pad.

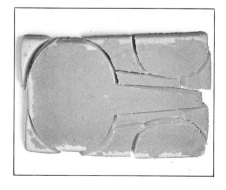

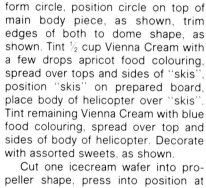

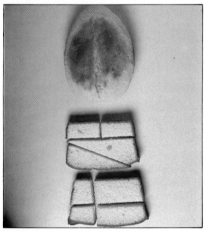

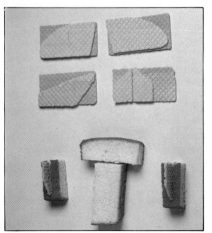

JET PLANE
1 packet butter cake mix
5 icecream wafers
1 quantity Vienna Cream
apricot food colouring
hundreds and thousands
assorted sweets (as shown)

Make cake according to directions on packet, pour into greased 23cm x 12cm (9in x 5in) loaf tin, bake in moderate oven 50 minutes or until cooked when tested. Turn cake on to wire rack to cool.

Cut 1cm (½in) slice from either end of cake, cut each slice into four, as shown; make a "T" with the two larger pieces from first slice to form base for body of plane. The two rectangular pieces from second slice are engine cowlings; use one triangular piece for top centre of plane. Shape main piece to form body of plane, as shown. Cut wafers, as shown, to make two wing pieces, one centre-tail piece, two side-tail pieces, plus two more pieces same size and shape as side-tail pieces for engine mount. Assemble cake on prepared board.

Tint Vienna Cream with a few drops apricot food colouring, cover top and sides of body with Vienna Cream, position on base, cover top and sides of triangular piece with Vienna Cream, coat with hundreds and thousands, place on top of body piece towards rear, as shown. Cover top and sides of engine cowlings with Vienna Cream, position, as shown; press in wafers. Press wings, side and centre tails in position, decorate cake with assorted sweets, as shown.

TUG BOAT

2 packets butter cake mix
thin licorice
toothpicks
1½ quantities Vienna Cream
yellow food colouring
green food colouring
orange or apricot food colouring
licorice allsorts
white Lifesavers
tubular licorice
1 licorice "bullet"
pipecleaners
toy flag
coloured popcorn

Make up cakes according to directions on packet, divide mixture evenly between two greased 28cm × 18cm (11in × 7in) lamington tins, bake in moderate oven 30 minutes or until cooked when tested. Turn on to wire racks to cool.

With a sharp knife, cut one cake, as shown, to form base layer of tug boat, cut other cake, as shown, to form middle and top layers. Assemble cake in layers, as shown. For wheel of boat, take a thin strip licorice, form into a circle, make spokes with toothpicks pressed firmly into licorice; if necessary, trim toothpicks, depending on size of circle (or wheel can be made from pipecleaners; see Horse Corral, page 126).

Divide Vienna Cream in half, tint one half with yellow food colouring; halve other portion, tint one quantity with green food colouring, tint the other quantity with orange or apricot food colouring. Cover base of tug smoothly with yellow cream, cover middle layer with green and top layer with orange. Cut licorice allsorts lengthwise into four, arrange around edge of boat, as shown, press Lifesavers on to middle layer to represent portholes. Cut tubular licorice into small rounds, arrange around top layer of boat, twist thin licorice in coil shape around "bullet" to represent rope in corner of bottom layer, wrap thin licorice twice around finger to represent tyres, twist pieces pipecleaner around tops of tyres, push ends of pipecleaners into edge of boat, as shown. Position flag, as shown, push skewer into middle of top layer, place tubular licorice over skewer to represent funnel. Make small holes in popcorn, thread on to pipecleaner, insert pipecleaner in funnel to represent smoke. Position wheel in centre of top layer, as shown.

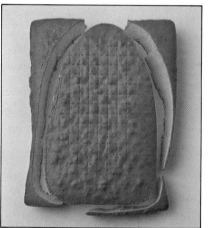

TIP TRUCK

2 packets butter cake mix
cardboard
aluminium foil
8 empty matchboxes
2 quantities Vienna Cream
egg-yellow food colouring (or
apricot or orange, as available)
green food colouring (not leaf-green)
blue food colouring
icing sugar
150g packet chocolate biscuit sticks
16 round chocolate biscuits
licorice
assorted sweets (as shown)
2 Lifesavers
toothpicks
sticky tape
1 board 50cm x 25cm (20in x 10in)

Make cakes according to directions on packet, divide evenly between two greased 23cm x 12cm (9in x 5in) loaf tins, bake in moderate oven 50 minutes or until cooked when tested. Turn on to wire rack to cool.

Invert both cakes, cut one in half horizontally, as shown; these two halves will form tray of truck. Trim sides of both cakes so they are flat, cut piece from second cake, as shown; cut-off piece forms support for tray, larger piece forms cabin. For tray of truck, cut 1cm (½in) recess in one half of cake, as shown. Cut piece of cardboard (cut-up breakfast cereal carton is ideal) same width as cake and 8cm (3in) longer, cover with aluminium foil, set aside. To make supporting wedge, invert piece cut from cabin so longer side is down; starting from uncut end of piece, cut diagonally to other side of cake, giving two wedge-shaped pieces, then cut top wedge into two pieces, as shown (smaller piece is not needed for truck). Two remaining wedges form support for tray of truck. Assemble cake on prepared board. Cover eight matchboxes with aluminium foil, position under cabin and body, as shown; arrange two wedge-shaped pieces slightly off centre on truck body, as shown (picture shows final assembly).

To colour Vienna Cream bright green, first tint brightly with up to 2 teaspoons egg-yellow food colouring, add about ½ teaspoon green food colouring, then add a few drops blue food colouring. This additional liquid will soften Vienna Cream, so beat in up to 1 cup extra sifted icing sugar to restore to correct consistency.

Cover body and cabin of truck with green Vienna Cream, position chocolate biscuit sticks behind cabin; join two round chocolate biscuits together with a little Vienna Cream to form dual wheels, repeat seven times. Outline windows, doors and windscreen with thin strips licorice, cut fine pieces

licorice for windscreen wipers and door handles; assorted sweets, as shown, represent headlights, grille, tail lights, mascot, fog horns; rear vision mirrors are Lifesavers wrapped in aluminium foil with toothpicks pushed into back of foil then into cake; two toothpicks joined with sticky tape and covered with aluminium foil represent CB radio aerial.

Cover top and sides of tray with green Vienna Cream, place on foil-covered cardboard, crease cardboard at each end, as shown, turn up creased ends, position on body of truck, fill cavity in tray with sweets.

FOR GIRLS

CANDY CASTLE

2 packets butter cake mix
4 icecream cones
1 quantity Fluffy Frosting (3 egg
**   white quantity)**
1 empty matchbox
assorted sweets (as shown)
1 icecream wafer
toothpicks

Make cakes together according to directions on packet, spoon one quarter of combined mixture into greased 25cm x 8cm (10in x 3in) bar tin, spoon remaining mixture into greased deep 20cm (8in) square cake tin, bake in moderate oven 30 minutes for bar cake, 1 hour for square cake or until cooked when tested. Turn on to wire rack to cool. If necessary, trim tops of cakes to give flat surfaces.

Place square cake on prepared board; cut bar cake into four equal pieces, position one piece on each corner of square cake, as shown, place an upside-down icecream cone in each corner. Cover cake and cones completely with Fluffy Frosting. Remove striker sides from matchbox cover, press one end lightly into frosting to form brick pattern. Decorate cake with assorted sweets, as shown; icecream wafer represents door, squares of soft fondant sweets on toothpicks represent flags on turrets (see Licorice Allsorts, page 3).

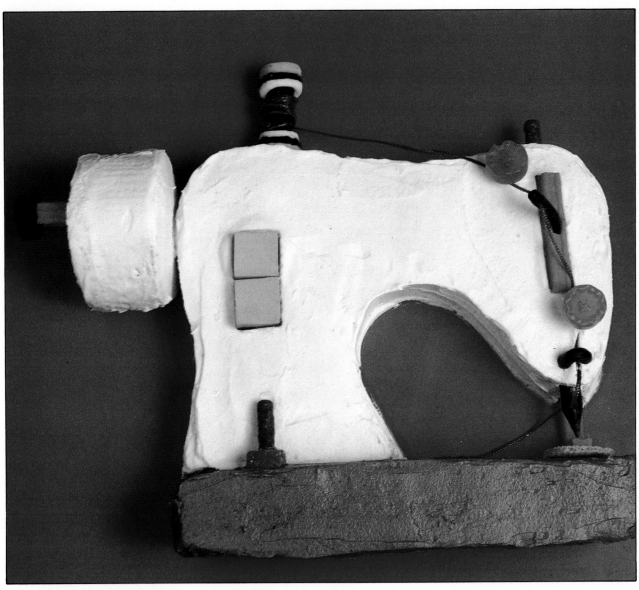

SEWING MACHINE

1 packet butter cake mix
1 quantity Vienna Cream
2 tablespoons cocoa
licorice
licorice allsorts
assorted sweets (as shown)
wooden cocktail sticks
cord
1 icecream wafer

Make cake according to directions on packet, pour into greased 23cm (9in) square slab tin, bake in moderate oven 30 minutes or until cooked when tested. Turn on to wire rack to cool.

Cut 5cm (2in) off bottom of cake to form base of machine. Trim remaining cake into the shape of the body of machine, as shown. From leftover piece cut a circle about 8cm (3in) in diameter, as shown, to make wheel. Place cake on prepared board. Tint ½ cup Vienna Cream with sifted cocoa, spread cream over top and sides of base, cover top and sides of body and wheel with the remaining Vienna Cream.

Assemble machine body on base, position wheel, as shown. Cottonreel is made by pressing 4cm (1½in) piece of thick licorice into two licorice allsorts. Decorate rest of machine with assorted sweets, as shown; if necessary, secure with wooden cocktail sticks. Wind coloured cord around cottonreel at top of machine, thread through and around sweets, as shown, thread through licorice needle. Plate under the needle is made from an icecream wafer trimmed to size.

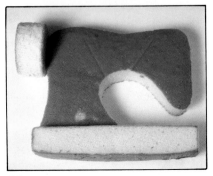

SEWING BASKET

1 packet butter cake mix
1½ quantities Vienna Cream
pink food colouring
2 tablespoons cocoa
chocolate "bullets"
silver cachous
bamboo skewers
2 musk sticks
chocolate sprinkles
wooden cocktail sticks
ribbons, lace, sewing aids (as shown)

Make cake according to directions on packet, place one tablespoon in a paper patty case to make pin cushion, pour remaining mixture into greased deep 20cm (8in) round cake tin, bake in moderate oven 10 to 15 minutes for patty cake, 50 minutes for round cake or until cooked when tested. Turn on to wire racks to cool. Tint half the Vienna Cream pale pink with food colouring, tint remaining Vienna Cream with sifted cocoa. Cut thin layer off top of cake about 1cm (½in) thick to make lid of basket, cut small piece off edge, as shown. Ice top of basket with pink Vienna Cream, spread chocolate Vienna Cream around sides, decorate sides with chocolate "bullets", as shown.

Spread edges and rounded side of lid with pink Vienna Cream, mark lightly with knife for quilted effect, press in silver cachous to give padded cushion appearance. With bamboo skewers, secure lid to back of basket; support lid with musk sticks, as shown. Carefully spread pink Vienna Cream over back of lid. Cover patty cake with chocolate Vienna Cream, coat with chocolate sprinkles, press wooden cocktail sticks into top to represent pins. When Vienna Cream is firm, decorate basket with ribbons, lace, scissors, thimble and buttons. If desired, small flat jubes can be used for buttons. Put small amount of chocolate Vienna Cream into corner of small paper bag (see How To Make Paper Piping Bags, page 4), pipe dots in centres of jubes to represent holes in buttons.

SWEETS SHOP

2 packets butter cake mix
1½ quantities Vienna Cream
pink food colouring
100g packet white chocolate
white cardboard
pink felt-tipped pen
1 packet candy sticks
licorice
small coloured sweets
1 iceblock stick
white paint
1 white marshmallow
2 small foil cases or milk bottle tops

Make cakes according to directions on packet, spoon one quarter of mixture into greased 25cm x 8cm (10in x 3in) bar tin, spoon remainder into deep 20cm (8in) square cake tin, bake in moderate oven 30 minutes for bar tin, 1 hour 10 minutes for square or until cooked when tested. Turn on to wire racks to cool.

Trim rounded tops off cakes. Stand square cake upright on prepared board, stand bar cake in front of it to represent front window and counter of shop. Cut 1cm (½in) recess in centre of square cake, as shown; cut 2.5cm (2in) recesses in either end of bar cake, as shown. Tint Vienna Cream pink with a few drops food colouring. Lie cake flat and ice front of window section first. Melt chocolate over simmering water, cool, pour into small paper bag (see page 4), pipe "Sweets Shop" on front.

When chocolate has set, stand cake up again and position behind counter. Ice remainder of cake evenly. Awning is made from white cardboard scalloped on the edge and striped with pink pen. Decorate window edge and counter front with candy sticks cut to shape. Use strips of licorice to trim awning and outline money drawer. Fill recesses in counter with coloured sweets; use coloured sweets for drawer handle. Scales are made by trimming ends off iceblock stick and painting it white; balance, when dry, across a white marshmallow. Trim two small foil cases or milk bottle tops and stick them at either end of iceblock stick with a little glue or sticky tape. Fill with sweets.

STOVE

1 packet butter cake mix
toothpicks
1 quantity Vienna Cream
green musk sticks
silver cachous
licorice
small piece fabric
sweets (as shown)
toy cooking utensils
1 white marshmallow
chocolate "bullets"
Jaffas
toy cups, saucers, plates

Make cake according to directions on packet, pour into greased 28cm x 18cm (11in x 7in) lamington tin, bake in moderate oven 30 minutes or until cooked when tested. Turn on to wire rack to cool. Cut cake, as shown; cut 10cm (4in) off each end of cake, leaving 8cm (3in) piece in centre.

Assemble cake, as follows, on prepared board: place one 10cm (4in) piece of cake on board, top with 8cm (3in) piece, place second 10cm (4in) piece on its side behind 8cm (3in)

piece, secure with toothpicks. If necessary, trim cakes so they're even. Cover cake evenly with Vienna Cream.

Cut musk sticks into thin strips, press on to edges of cake, as shown. Arrange cachous, as shown, to represent oven door; press thin strip of licorice into icing at the two top ends of door to represent handle. Cut small piece of fabric into rectangle, carefully hang it over door handle to represent teatowel. Press coloured sweets on to splashback to represent dials. Wind licorice into tight coils to represent hotplates, place on top of stove, add cooking equipment.

To make eggs, halve a marshmallow, flatten slightly, then place yellow sweets in centres. Chocolate "bullets" represent sausages, Jaffas in saucepan represent tomatoes. To hang remaining kitchen equipment, push toothpicks into either side of stove. Arrange cups, saucers and plates along top of stove, as shown.

BALLERINAS

4 packets butter cake mix
wooden skewers
2 quantities Vienna Cream
red food colouring
1 card or picture for backdrop
gold cachous
small fabric or plastic flowers
ballet dancer dolls
candle holders
candles
fabric for curtains

Make cakes according to directions on packet, divide mixture between greased deep 23cm (9in) square cake tin and greased deep 20cm (8in) round cake tin, making sure mixture is the same depth in each tin, bake in moderate oven 1 hour for round cake, 1¼ hours for square or until cooked when tested. Turn cakes on to wire rack to cool.

With a sharp knife, cut out a deep rectangle from one end of square cake, as shown; do not cut right through cake, leave 4cm (1½in) border all round. Assemble cakes, as shown, on prepared board; if necessary, insert long wooden skewers through centre of square cake into round cake to hold firm. Tint Vienna Cream pink with a few drops red food colouring, ice round cake with Vienna Cream; spread sufficient Vienna Cream on square cake for backdrop picture to adhere. Choose a card or picture with a pretty scene, position on square cake, as shown.

Place rest of Vienna Cream in piping bag fitted with a small star shaped tube; pipe small bands of stars around top and bottom edges of round cake, pipe a decorative pattern around side of cake, decorate with gold cachous and flowers, as shown. Arrange dancers on top of cake, position candle holders between dancers, cut candles in half, insert in candle holders, preferably at the front to represent footlights, place cachous around candles; fill rest of holders with flowers. Make curtain; if necessary, sew a running thread through top of each curtain drop to gather slightly. Position on cake, as shown, secure with a little Vienna Cream.

For a simpler cake, the back can be omitted and a cake made of the stage only. For this, only two packets of cake mix are required. Pour them into a deep 23cm (9in) round cake tin, bake in moderate oven 1¼ hours or until cooked when tested. You will still need two quantities of Vienna Cream.

Note: Several types of ballerina dolls are available from most cake shops and shops which specialize in cake-decorating equipment.

DRESSING TABLE

2 packets butter cake mix
jam
1 quantity Vienna Cream
1 metre gingham or other fabric
ribbon
toy "vanity" items

Make cakes according to directions on packet, divide evenly between two greased 28cm x 18cm (11in x 7in) lamington tins, bake in moderate oven 30 minutes or until cooked when tested. Turn on to wire rack to cool.

When cold, place one cake on top of the other, cut carefully into dressing table shape, as shown. Cut circular piece about 6cm (2½in) in diameter from scraps to represent stool, cut a slice about 2.5cm (1in) deep from top of stool to make it slightly lower than dressing table. Join cake pieces together with jam and a little Vienna Cream, assemble on prepared board, spread dressing table and stool with remaining Vienna Cream, making tops as smooth as possible. Cut two strips

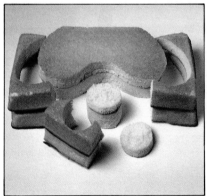

of fabric about 9cm (3½in) wide from each selvedge, cut one strip in half crossways. Sew the long piece of fabric to one short piece to make it longer, tack right along the length of this strip about 1cm (½in) down from selvedge, then cut strip to depth of dressing table, trim with pinking shears for a neat edge. Draw tacking thread to fit fabric around dressing table, press gathered edge lightly on to Vienna Cream (fabric should stay in position quite easily). Sew two small ribbon bows on to skirt, as shown. Use remaining short piece of fabric to make skirt about 6cm (2½in) deep for stool. Arrange toys on top of cake.

Note: Fabric will begin to absorb a little fat from the butter after several hours.

MAYPOLE

1 packet butter cake mix
1 quantity Vienna Cream
green food colouring
2 cups coconut
long candy stick
small dolls
brightly coloured ribbons
1 drawing pin
artificial flowers
coloured sweets (as shown)

Make cake according to directions on packet, pour into greased deep 20cm (8in) round cake tin, bake in moderate oven 50 minutes or until cooked when tested. Turn on to wire rack to cool. Tint Vienna Cream with a few drops green food colouring, cover top and sides with green-tinted coconut. Push candy stick into centre of cake, arrange dolls evenly around edge. Tie one piece of ribbon in a bow around each waist, attach ends to top of candy stick, as shown, with a drawing pin. Tie a bow around artificial flowers, place on top of maypole, secure with Vienna Cream. Arrange coloured sweets in a pattern around side of cake.

BASKET OF FLOWERS

1 packet butter cake mix
1 quantity Vienna Cream
green food colouring
2 cups green-tinted coconut
marshmallow flowers (see page 4)
round flat sweets
jube rings
aluminium foil
ribbon

Make cake according to directions on packet, spoon mixture evenly into greased deep 23cm (9in) round cake tin, bake in moderate oven 45 minutes or until cooked when tested. Turn on to wire rack to cool. Tint Vienna Cream with a few drops green food colouring, spread evenly over top and side of cake, sprinkle with green-tinted coconut to cover cream.

Decorate edge of the cake with marshmallow flowers, as shown, press halved jubes into cake to form a ring just inside marshmallow flowers. To make a handle, roll a 40cm (16in) square of aluminium foil into a strip, twist for a firm finish, attach ribbon bow, insert handle in cake, as shown.

CAKE OF KISSES

8 egg whites (large size is essential)
2 cups castor sugar
1 or 2 drops pink food colouring
3 x 300ml cartons thickened cream
aluminium foil

Cover two large flat oven trays or scone trays with aluminium foil. On first tray mark two circles, one 15cm (6in), one 10cm (4in) in diameter. On second tray mark three circles, 12cm (5in), 8cm (3in) and 5cm (2in) in diameter. (Saucers, cups, jars or lids of the right sizes can be used as guides.) The meringues are made in two batches, one using five egg whites, the other using three egg whites. Before making second batch, cover the trays with fresh aluminium foil.

Beat three egg whites in small bowl of electric mixer until soft peaks form, gradually beat in ¾ cup sugar, 1 tablespoon at a time. Make sure each spoon of sugar is dissolved by beating before adding the next spoon, as this ensures crisp meringues. If you want pink layers in cake, beat in enough food colouring to tint meringue light pink. Spoon meringue into large piping bag fitted with 2cm (¾in) plain tube, pipe mixture over circles marked on foil on the two prepared trays, pipe another layer of meringue on top so that each circle is 2cm (¾in) thick, smooth tops of circles with spatula. Bake in very slow oven 1¼ to 1½ hours, reversing oven position of trays after 30 minutes to allow for even cooking. When meringue feels dry to touch, remove from oven and carefully slide foil with meringue circles on top on to wire rack. If time permits, let meringues cool in oven with door ajar before sliding foil with meringue circles on to wire rack.

Prepare three trays as before for remaining meringues; mark 18cm (7in) circle on one tray. Prepare second batch of meringue, as above, with remaining five egg whites and 1¼ cups sugar but no colouring; beat egg whites in large bowl of electric mixer. With piping bag and 2cm (¾in) plain tube, pipe a single layer of meringue over 18cm (7in) circle to a thickness of 1cm (½in); pipe 14 individual meringues 4cm (1½in) in diameter on to foil. Use remaining mixture to pipe small individual meringues 2.5cm (1in) in diameter on to remaining foil-covered trays (you will need about 60 small meringues).

Bake in very slow oven. Approximate cooking times are as follows (meringues should be cooked until they are firm and crisp): meringue circles — 1 to 1½ hours; 4cm (1½in) meringues — 1 hour; 2.5cm (1in) meringues — 30 to 45 minutes. When cooking the tray holding the 18cm

circle and 14 4cm (1½in) meringues, remove from oven after 1 hour, slide individual meringues on to wire rack, return circle to oven for remainder of cooking time. Two trays can be cooked at the same time; reverse positions in oven after half the cooking time to ensure that all the meringues cook evenly.

Whip cream to firm piping consistency, spoon into large piping bag fitted with star tube. Place 18cm (7in) meringue circle on serving plate,

spread top lightly with whipped cream, top with 15cm (6in) circle; add layers of cream topped with rest of meringue circles in diminishing order of size. Pipe a small star of cream on the back of each meringue as you position it. Gently press 4cm (1½in) diameter individual meringues around base of cake, press circle of small meringues into place above these; continue in this way until all small meringues are used. Pipe small stars of cream between assembled meringues.

CAKE OF HEARTS
MERINGUE HEARTS
2 egg whites
½ cup castor sugar
greaseproof paper
hundreds and thousands
CAKE
1 packet sponge cake mix
strawberry or other jam
2 x 300ml cartons cream

Meringue Hearts: Beat egg whites until soft peaks form, gradually beat in castor sugar, beat until firm peaks form. Grease and flour a sheet of greaseproof paper, place on baking tray, trace small heart shapes lightly on to paper with a pencil. Put 1 teaspoon meringue mixture on to each heart, spread into heart shape, as shown. Sprinkle with hundreds and thousands, press these on lightly with small spatula, bake in slow oven 20 minutes or until firm to touch. There is sufficient meringue mixture for about 12 hearts (you could have one for each year of the child's age).

Cake: Make cake according to directions on packet, spread evenly into greased 25cm (10in) heart-shaped cake tin, bake in moderate oven 30 minutes or until cake shrinks slightly from sides of tin. If preferred, cake can be baked in 20cm (8in) round cake tin for 20 to 25 minutes, then cut into heart shape when cold. Turn on to wire rack to cool.

Cut cake in half horizontally, then rejoin with thin layers of jam and whipped cream, cover top and sides with whipped cream, press meringue hearts into position around cake, as shown, pipe a decorative border of cream around top edge of cake.

DOLLY VARDEN

1 packet butter cake mix
1 doll
1 quantity Vienna Cream
3 x 100g packets marshmallows
1 metre ribbon
artificial flower

Make cake according to directions on packet, pour into well-greased Dolly Varden tin, bake in moderate oven 1 hour or until cooked when tested. Turn on to wire rack to cool.

Gently push doll down into cake, cover cake with Vienna Cream. Halve marshmallows (if you dip scissors blades in water, marshmallows will cut easily). A combination of pink and white marshmallows, as shown, looks attractive. Press marshmallows, cut side down, all over "skirt", starting from the bottom. Wind ribbon around doll's body to represent bodice, tie at back in large bow, position artificial flower at waist.

Note: For information on Dolly Varden tins, see page 5.

TEA PARTY
1 packet butter cake mix
1 quantity Vienna Cream
purple food colouring
12 chocolate Freckles
5 icecream wafers
dolls' teaset
4 round sweets
hundreds and thousands
four small dolls

Make cake according to directions on packet, pour into greased 28cm x 18cm (11in x 7in) lamington tin, bake in moderate oven 30 minutes or until cooked when tested. Turn on to wire rack to cool.

Using saucer as guide, cut 15cm (6in) round from cake for table; with 5cm (2in) plain cutter, cut four stools from remaining cake. Tint 2 tablespoons Vienna Cream dark mauve with purple food colouring, tint remainder light mauve, cover tops and sides of table and stools with light mauve Vienna Cream. Decorate top edge of table with halved Freckles. Cut four wafers with 5cm (2in) plain cutter to make place mats, cut remaining wafer with 4cm (1½in) plain cutter to make mat for centre of table. Pipe dark mauve Vienna Cream along cut edges of mats (see page 4), place in position, as shown, arrange teaset on mats, add round sweets. Coat stools with hundreds and thousands, press dolls' feet into stools.

DANCING GIRL

1 butter cake mix
2 quantities Vienna Cream
pink food colouring
raspberry jam
1 doll
small sweets (as shown)
silver cachous
small piece pink ribbon

Make up mixture, pour evenly into two greased 20cm (8in) sandwich tins, bake in moderate oven 25 to 30 minutes or until cooked when tested. Turn on to wire racks to cool.

Tint 1½ quantities of Vienna Cream with pink food colouring. Join cakes together with a little raspberry jam, trim top to give shape to dress, as shown.

Place doll in centre of cake; if doll is too tall, trim legs. Place pink cream in piping bag fitted with star-shaped tube, pipe decoratively over chest to form bodice of dress, pipe cream in a scallop formation over top of skirt. With white Vienna Cream, pipe around bottom of cake and up sides of scallops to form the underskirt.

Decorate top with a few rosettes of white cream; decorate skirt with small sweets. Using tweezers, dip silver cachous into a little icing, then place around doll's wrist to form silver bangle. Repeat process with shoulder straps. Place a little icing on the backs of two small sweets, place on ribbon headband to form flowers.

MARY JANE

2 packets butter cake mix
small skewers
2 quantities Vienna Cream
pink food colouring
yellow food colouring
blue food colouring
green food colouring
brown food colouring
4 packets Lifesavers
125g (4oz) shredded coconut
licorice
glace cherries
ribbon
1 board 68cm x 30cm (27in x 12in)

Make cakes according to directions on packet, pour just over half into greased 28cm x 18cm (11in x 7in) lamington tin, pour remainder into greased 18cm (7in) round sandwich tin, bake in moderate oven 25 to 30 minutes or until cooked when tested. Turn on to wire rack to cool.

Cut out cakes, as shown (cake in lamington tin makes body, arms, legs and feet, round cake makes head and bonnet). Assemble cake, as shown, on prepared board, securing bonnet with small skewers. Divide Vienna Cream into six bowls; tint one with a few drops pink food colouring, second with a few drops yellow food colouring, third with a few drops blue food colouring, fourth with a few drops green food colouring, fifth with a few drops brown food colouring; leave sixth plain.

Spread plain cream thinly over face, arms, legs and body. Spread patches of coloured cream thickly to give patchwork effect on skirt, bib, straps and bonnet. Colour shoes with one plain colour. Cut Lifesavers in half, press them into the plain cream at top of body to give crochet effect. If desired, coloured Lifesavers can be used for lace edge of sleeves. Tint coconut with a drop of pink food colouring, press on to plain area of arms and legs. Decorate face, as shown, with licorice strips for hair, eyebrows and expression lines, use pieces of glace cherries for eyes, cheeks, nose and mouth, press bows of ribbon on shoes and around neck.

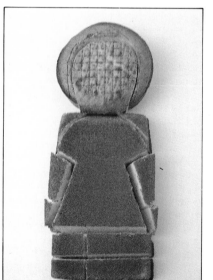

BABY IN BASKET

1 packet butter cake mix
1 quantity Vienna Cream
pink food colouring
lace
small piece fabric
baby doll
pipecleaners
pink ribbon

Make cake according to directions on packet, pour into greased 23cm x 12cm (9in x 5in) loaf tin, bake in moderate oven 50 minutes or until cooked when tested. Turn cake on to wire rack to cool.

With sharp knife, trim top of cake to make it even, trim corners to round them, scoop out hollow about 2cm (¾in) in from edge, as shown. Tint Vienna Cream with a few drops pink food colouring, cover outside and edge of cake with Vienna Cream (do not ice hollow). Edge neatly with lace, as shown, make pillow, place in basket, place doll in hollow, tuck in coverlet. Twist pipecleaners together, cover with ribbon, push into sides of cake to form handles, tie a bow at each end.

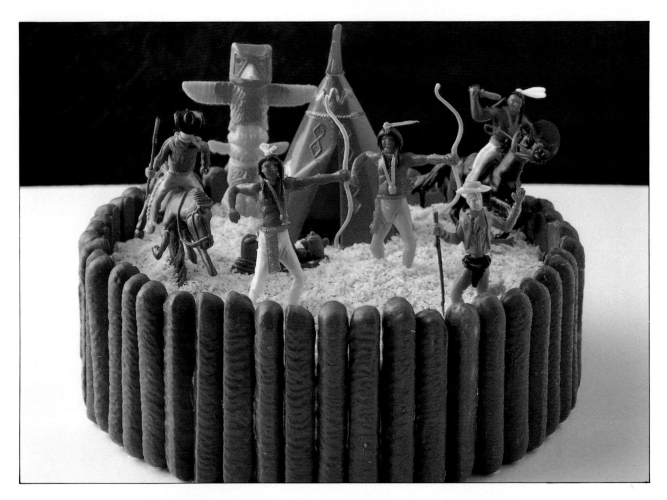

THREE EASY CAKES

Just by changing the toys on top, you can make a simple round cake look quite different. All toys shown are available from supermarkets or toy departments of large stores. Most farmyard sets include a gate, otherwise you can make one by placing chocolate biscuit sticks horizontally across the opening in the fence.

COWBOYS AND INDIANS
1 packet butter cake mix
1 quantity Vienna Cream
1 cup coconut
green food colouring
2 x 150g packets chocolate
  biscuit sticks
1 packet toy cowboys and Indians
Make cake according to directions on packet, pour into greased deep 20cm (8in) round cake tin, bake in moderate oven 50 minutes or until cooked when tested. Turn on to wire rack to cool.

Tint Vienna Cream and coconut with a few drops green food colouring, cover top and sides of cake with Vienna Cream, sprinkle top with green-tinted coconut. Stand chocolate biscuit sticks around cake to represent fence. Arrange toys on top of cake.

ZOO
1 packet butter cake mix
1 quantity Vienna Cream
1 cup coconut
green food colouring
2 x 150g packets chocolate
  biscuit sticks
blue paper
chocolates
round brown sweets
1 packet plastic zoo animals
Make cake according to directions on packet, pour into greased deep 20cm (8in) round cake tin, bake in moderate oven 50 minutes or until cooked when tested. Turn on to wire rack to cool.

Tint Vienna Cream and coconut with a few drops green food colouring, cover top and sides of cake with Vienna Cream, sprinkle top with green-tinted coconut. Stand chocolate biscuit sticks vertically around cake to represent fence. Cut blue paper into small round to represent pond. Scatter chocolates and sweets around pond to represent rocks. Arrange zoo animals and tree on top of cake.
Note: Blue paper kindergarten squares are ideal for the pond and are available at most newsagencies.

FARMYARD
1 packet butter cake mix
1 quantity Vienna Cream
1 cup coconut
green food colouring
2 x 150g packets chocolate
  biscuit sticks
blue paper
1 packet plastic farm animals
chocolate "bullets"
Make cake according to directions on packet, pour into greased deep 20cm (8in) round cake tin, bake in moderate oven 50 minutes or until cooked when tested. Turn on to wire rack to cool.

Tint Vienna Cream and coconut with a few drops green food colouring, cover top and sides of cake with Vienna Cream, sprinkle top with green-tinted coconut. Stand chocolate biscuit sticks vertically around cake to represent fence, leaving a small opening for gate. Cut blue paper into small round, place on cake to represent pond. Arrange farm animals and tree on cake, scatter a few chocolate "bullets" to represent logs.
Note: Blue paper kindergarten squares are ideal for the pond and are available at most newsagencies.

LOVE ME EVER
Words by Jackie....Music by

E FOR EVERYONE

PIANO
2 packets butter cake mix
1½ quantities chocolate
**   Vienna Cream**
2 x 150g blocks white chocolate
licorice
1 icecream wafer
small piece cardboard
birthday candles

Make cakes according to directions on packet, spoon one quarter into greased 25cm x 8cm (10in x 3in) bar tin, spoon remaining mixture into greased deep 20cm (8in) square cake tin, bake in moderate oven 30 to 35 minutes for bar cake, 1 hour 10 minutes for square or until cooked when tested. Turn on to wire racks to cool.

Cut 2.5cm (1in) slice off one side of square cake, stand cake on end to form back of piano. If necessary, trim sides of bar cake; cut one end off bar cake to make it the same length as back of piano, position in front of other cake, as shown, to form keyboard. Using a 4cm (1½in) round cutter, cut a circle from cut-off piece of bar cake to make piano stool; cut a piece from base of stool so it is lower than keyboard. Place on board.

Ice both piano and stool with the Vienna Cream. Cut chocolate into 5cm (2in) strips, place upside down along keyboard, as shown, to represent white keys. Cut licorice strips 4cm (1½in) long, place along keyboard, as shown, to represent black keys. Trim icecream wafer into rectangle 5cm x 4cm (2in x 1½in), press into back of piano, as shown, to represent music stand. Sheet music can be cut out and pasted on to small piece cardboard. Add candelabra (or other small toy).

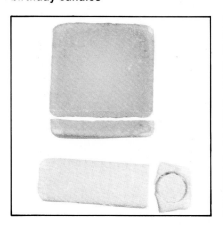

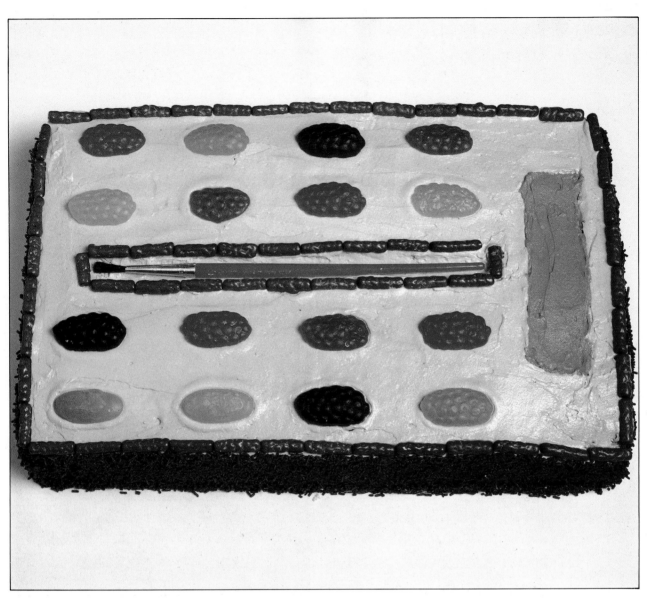

PAINT BOX

1 packet butter cake mix
1 quantity Vienna Cream
1 tablespoon instant coffee powder
1 teaspoon hot water
paint brush
fruit jubes
blue food colouring
chocolate "bullets"
chocolate sprinkles

Make cake according to directions on packet, spoon evenly into greased 28cm x 18cm (11in x 7in) lamington tin, bake in moderate oven 30 minutes or until cooked when tested. Turn on to wire rack to cool.

Reserve 2 tablespoons Vienna Cream; dissolve coffee powder in hot water, cool, add to remaining Vienna Cream, beat well. Cut a groove out of centre of cake the same length and a little wider than brush, as shown, for brush holder. Cut a rectangle 2.5cm (1in) wide, 10cm (4in) long, 1cm (½in) deep out of one end of cake, as shown, to form water container. Cover cake evenly with coffee Vienna Cream, arrange fruit jubes over top of cake to represent paints. Tint 2 tablespoons Vienna Cream with a few drops blue food colouring, spread evenly into water container. Line edge of cake with chocolate "bullets", coat sides with chocolate sprinkles, as shown. Position paint brush.

ARTIST'S PALETTE
1 packet butter cake mix
1 quantity Vienna Cream
3 tablespoons cocoa
assorted food colourings (as shown)
2 paint brushes

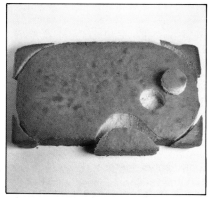

Make cake according to directions on packet, pour into greased 28cm x 18cm (11in x 7in) lamington tin, bake in moderate oven 30 minutes or until cooked when tested. Turn on to wire rack to cool.

Cut cake, as shown. Combine two thirds Vienna Cream with sifted cocoa, mix well, cover top and sides of cake with chocolate Vienna Cream. Tint 2 teaspoons plain Vienna Cream with a few drops one food colouring, repeat with remaining cream and each of chosen food colourings. With metal spatula, place coloured creams on cake to represent blobs of paint, as shown. If desired, a greeting can be written with leftover cream. Position paint brushes, as shown.

BLACKBOARD

2 packets butter cake mix
1 quantity Vienna Cream
red food colouring
1½ tablespoons instant
  coffee powder
2 teaspoons hot water
licorice
chocolate "bullets"

125g (4oz) dark chocolate
30g (1oz) Copha
assorted coloured musk sticks
large rectangular sweets
1 board 50cm x 35cm (20in x 14in)

Make cakes according to directions on packet, pour half into greased 28cm x 18cm (11in x 7in) lamington tin, pour other half into greased 23cm x 12cm (9in x 5in) loaf tin, bake in moderate oven 30 minutes for lamington tin cake, 50 minutes for loaf or until cooked when tested. Turn on to wire racks to cool.

Cut shallow recess about 3mm (⅛in) deep 1cm (½in) in from edge of lamington tin cake, as shown, to make frame and recess of blackboard. Cut two 4cm x 18cm (1½in x 7in) strips from loaf cake for legs, cut 6cm x 4cm (2½in x 1½in) rectangle for top, assemble, as shown, on prepared board. Tint one third cup Vienna Cream with a

few drops red food colouring; combine coffee powder with water, add to remaining Vienna Cream, mix well. Spread legs and frame with coffee Vienna Cream. Use licorice for bar which joins legs of blackboard, decorate frame with chocolate "bullets". Put chopped chocolate and Copha in top of double saucepan, stir over simmering water until melted, cool; pour chocolate mixture into recess of blackboard, spread evenly, allow to set. Fill small paper bag (see page 4) with pink Vienna Cream, pipe greeting on blackboard. Pieces of coloured musk sticks represent chalks, rectangular sweet represents duster.

114

The image shows a typewriter cake with "Happy Birthday" on a sheet of paper in the roller.

TYPEWRITER

2 packets butter cake mix
1 quantity Vienna Cream
apricot food colouring
blue food colouring
2 round chocolate biscuits
musk sticks
thin licorice
small round sweets

Make cakes according to directions on packet, pour into greased deep 23cm (9in) square cake tin, bake in moderate oven 1 to 1¼ hours or until cooked when tested. Turn on to wire rack to cool.

Cut a slit straight down 2.5cm (1in) in from back edge, halfway through cake; cut a similar slit 5cm (2in) away from first slit, halfway through cake. Carve centre piece between slits into a semi-cylindrical shape to represent roller. Starting 9cm (3½in) from front edge, cut a slice at an angle sloping towards the front. With a small knife, cut triangular recess between keyboard and roller. Assemble, as shown, on prepared board.

Tint 4 tablespoons Vienna Cream with apricot food colouring; tint remaining Vienna Cream with blue food colouring. Cover cylinder and keyboard with apricot Vienna Cream, cover rest of top and sides with blue Vienna Cream, leaving the triangular recess plain. Put chocolate biscuits on either end of roller; use musk sticks for handle, typewriter ribbon inside recess and spacing bar. Line bottom of recess with thin strips licorice to represent arms of keys; small round sweets pushed into icing at a slight angle represent keys. If desired, slip coloured paper lettered with "Happy Birthday" on either side of roller just before serving.

TELEVISION

2 packets butter cake mix
1½ quantities chocolate
**   Vienna Cream**
birthday card
thick cardboard
chocolate "bullets"
small round sweets
licorice
licorice allsorts

Make cakes according to directions on packet, spoon evenly into greased deep 23cm (9in) square cake tin, bake in moderate oven 1 hour 15 minutes

until cooked when tested. Turn on to wire rack to cool.

Trim rounded top off cake, as shown, cut cake in half, trim sides off rounded top to fit evenly on top of one half to form main part of television set. Cut 1cm (½in) recess in centre of other half, as shown, invert to form base and legs of set. Place on prepared board. Stand other half on base, as shown, add trimmed rounded top. Cover cake completely with chocolate Vienna Cream.

To make screen, mount a wide cutout birthday card, about 15cm x 9cm (6in x 3½in), on piece thick cardboard, curve corners with scissors. Position screen on front of cake, border with chocolate "bullets"; round sweets, licorice strips and licorice allsorts cut into triangles represent dials.

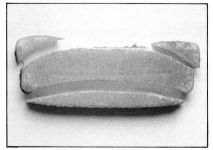

TELEPHONE

2 packets butter cake mix
1 quantity Vienna Cream
purple food colouring
pink food colouring
silver cachous
chocolate "bullets"
coloured Lifesavers
hundreds and thousands
small round sweets
licorice

Make cakes according to directions on packet, pour enough to half fill greased 25cm x 8cm (10in x 3in) bar tin, pour enough of remaining mixture to half fill deep 20cm (8in) square cake tin, bake in moderate oven 30 minutes for bar cake, 55 minutes for square cake or until cooked when tested. Turn on to wire racks to cool. (Make patty cakes with any leftover mixture.)

Trim both cakes so they are equal in height. With a small sharp knife, cut two rounded corners from top of square cake for earpiece and mouthpiece, as shown. Trim bar cake into a curve. Assemble cake, as shown, on prepared board. Tint ⅓ cup Vienna Cream with a few drops of purple food colouring, tint rest of Vienna Cream with pink food colouring, cover earpiece and mouthpiece with purple Vienna Cream, cover rest of cake with pink Vienna Cream.

Scatter silver cachous on inside of earpiece and mouthpiece, push ends of chocolate "bullets" into main part of cake to form circle, press coloured Lifesavers on to "bullets" to represent dial. Sprinkle inside of dial with hundreds and thousands, place small round sweets in centre to form small circle, as shown. Push "bullets" into cake where receiver meets body of telephone. Wrap licorice strap tightly around pencil, remove pencil, use licorice to represent cord of telephone, as shown.

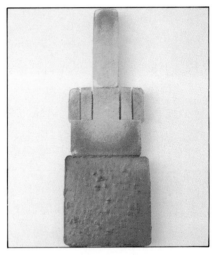

GUITAR

2 packets butter cake mix
1 quantity Vienna Cream
4 tablespoons cocoa
thin licorice
1 icecream wafer

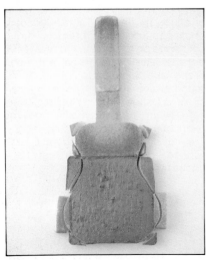

2 musk sticks
hat elastic
1 piece thick licorice
6 lollipops
1 metre 5cm (2in) wide ribbon
1 board 83cm x 38cm (33in x 15in)

Make cakes according to directions on packet, half fill greased 25cm x 8cm (10in x 3in) bar tin, divide remaining mixture evenly between greased deep 20cm (8in) square cake tin and deep 23cm (9in) square cake tin, so that cake mixture is the same depth in each, bake in moderate oven 30 minutes for bar cake, 40 to 45 minutes for square cakes or until cooked when tested. Turn on to wire racks to cool.

Assemble the three cakes, as shown, on prepared board, placing bar cake in centre at end of smaller square cake. Make two slits in top of each side of smaller square cake, as shown, to halfway through cake; cut off these four small pieces (you will need only two cut-out pieces for the guitar). Place one cut-out piece on

either side of 23cm (9in) square cake 4cm (1½in) up from bottom, cut cake into shape of guitar, as shown.

Tint 5 tablespoons Vienna Cream with 3 tablespoons sifted cocoa, cover top and sides of neck and define sound hole with chocolate Vienna Cream. Tint rest of Vienna Cream with remaining 1 tablespoon cocoa, cover top and sides of rest of cake with this Vienna Cream. Edge sound hole with piece thin licorice, arrange pieces thin licorice across neck, as shown. Cut wafer in half lengthwise, cut away two corners of each half, press wafer halves firmly into position, one to form bridge, the other at base of neck. Cut each musk stick crosswise into three, secure piece of elastic on each piece musk stick, press musk sticks well into top of neck, as shown. Press piece thick licorice firmly over elastic ends to hold steady. Position lollipops at top of neck, as shown, to represent tuning knobs; slip ends of ribbon into cake, as shown.

HOPSCOTCH

1 packet butter cake mix
1 quantity Vienna Cream
coloured sprinkles (as shown)
chocolate sprinkles
licorice
coloured pipecleaners (as shown)
1 board 50cm x 25cm (20in x 10in)

Make cake according to directions on packet, pour into greased 28cm x 18cm (11in x 7in) lamington tin, bake in moderate oven 30 minutes or until cooked when tested. Turn on to wire rack to cool.

Cut cake crosswise into five equal pieces, cut one end piece into dome shape, halve each of remaining four pieces, as shown, to give eight equal pieces. Take scrap cut from top piece of cake, place top edges together, trim to small dome, as shown, to go at bottom end of cake.

Cover top and sides of each piece of cake with the Vienna Cream, coat thoroughly with different coloured sprinkles and chocolate sprinkles, as shown, decorate with numbers made from licorice and pipecleaners (use light-coloured pipecleaners on pieces covered with chocolate sprinkles so that numbers will stand out clearly). Assemble pieces, as shown, on prepared board.

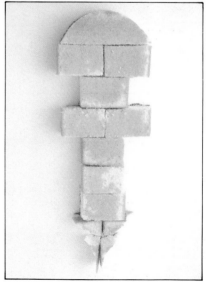

ROCKING HORSE

1 packet butter cake mix
1 quantity Vienna Cream
red food colouring
shredded coconut
assorted sweets (as shown)
1 large packet potato straws
licorice
silver cachous
4 wooden coathangers
1 board 60cm x 50cm (24in x 20in)

Make cake according to directions on packet, pour into greased 28cm x 18cm (11in x 7in) lamington tin, bake in moderate oven 30 minutes or until cooked when tested. Turn on to wire rack to cool.

Cut 4cm (1½in) wide strip from long edge of cake at base, cut this strip into three even-sized pieces; cut a small wedge from one third, as shown, for the ears, the larger wedge makes the head. Cut another wedge from the next third of cake; the small wedge makes the nose, the larger wedge makes the neck where it joins

the body. Cut about one third off the end of the remaining piece of cake; the larger piece forms the top part of the neck, discard the small piece. Cut a strip 4cm (1½in) wide from each end of cake for the legs; cut a slightly curved piece from one long side to give body shape. Assemble on prepared board, using leftover cake to fill gaps between legs and body.

Tint Vienna Cream with red food colouring, spread evenly over cake, sprinkle shredded coconut all over rocking horse. Small round sweets represent saddle and feet, potato straws pushed into horse's neck represent mane, tail is made from potato straws. Licorice strip and semicircle of silver cachous represent stirrup, long licorice strip represents bridle. Cut coloured jubes, as shown, to represent eyebrow, mouth and part of eye; small round sweet topped with tiny round sweet complete eye. Four coathangers, stacked two on top of each other, form the rocker.

LOG CABIN

2 packets butter cake mix
1 quantity Vienna Cream
250g (8oz) coconut
pink food colouring
green food colouring
assorted sweets (as shown)
licorice
6 Flake chocolates
small wooden skewers

Make cakes according to directions on packet, pour into greased deep 23cm (9in) square cake tin, bake in moderate oven 1¼ hours or until cooked when tested. Turn on to wire rack to cool.

Cut cake in half vertically, trim one half, as shown, to form roof, cut out chimney and tree from trimmings, assemble cake, as shown, on prepared board. Cover house with Vienna Cream. Tint 1½ cups coconut with a few drops pink food colouring, tint remaining coconut green. Coat walls with pink coconut. Make windows, gutters and doors out of small sweets and licorice strips, as shown. Cut Flakes into various lengths, place on roof, leaving a small space for window; fill in window with small sweets. Ice chimney with Vienna Cream, coat in Flake crumbs, place on side of house, secure with small wooden skewers. Ice tree with Vienna Cream, coat in green coconut, position near front door. Small sweets and jubes represent flowers; spread remaining green-tinted coconut around house, small round sweets represent garden path.

CANDLE
3 eggs
½ cup castor sugar
1 cup self-raising flour
3 tablespoons hot water
greaseproof paper
jam
1 quantity Fluffy Frosting (2 egg
**   white quantity)**
birthday candle
candy mint leaves
small round sweets

Beat eggs until thick and creamy, gradually add sugar, beat until sugar is dissolved, fold in sifted flour, stir in hot water, pour into greased greased-paper lined 35cm x 25cm (14in x 10in) swiss roll tin, bake in moderate oven 12 to 15 minutes or until cooked when tested. Turn on to sheet of grease-proof paper.

With a sharp knife, trim off crisp edges from long sides. With help of greaseproof paper, roll up, allow to cool. When cool, unwrap gently, spread with jam, carefully roll up again. Cut top off swiss roll at an angle, as shown, stand swiss roll on board or plate, spread with prepared frosting; with knife or handle of spoon, smear frosting down sides of cake for melting candle effect. Press candle into top of cake, decorate around base with mint leaves and small round sweets, surround with small sweets.
Note: This cake is best made the day before you want to ice it.

JACK IN THE BOX
1 packet butter cake mix
1 quantity Vienna Cream
red food colouring
blue food colouring
1 icecream cone
hundreds and thousands
coloured paper
licorice
2 icecream wafers
green musk sticks
assorted sweets (as shown)

Make cake according to directions on packet, pour into greased 23cm x 12cm (9in x 5in) loaf tin, bake in moderate oven 50 minutes or until cooked when tested. Turn cake on to wire rack to cool.

Trim cake until all sides are straight, stand cake on one end, press a 4cm (1½in) plain round cutter down through centre of cake as far as it will go; with a sharp knife, cut away cake from around outside of cutter, remove cutter. Press a 5cm (2in) plain cutter further down into cake, cut away cake from around outside of cutter to make second round. Trim sharp edges to make head and body where two rounds meet, leave top flat.

Reserve 3 tablespoons Vienna Cream, tint half remaining Vienna Cream with red food colouring, tint other half with blue food colouring. Cover sides of head and body with plain Vienna Cream, cover front, top and back of box with red Vienna Cream, cover remaining two sides with blue Vienna Cream. Cover pointed end of icecream cone with plain Vienna Cream, coat with hundreds and thousands, position on top of cake. Cut coloured paper to make collar, press into position. Wrap licorice strip around cake at join of body and box. Press wafers upright into top back edge of cake to form lid. Split musk sticks in half lengthwise, decorate all edges with prepared musk sticks, using plain Vienna Cream if necessary to make them adhere. Use small sweets, as shown, to represent facial features; decorate sides of box, as shown.

CHOO-CHOO TRAIN

2 packets butter cake mix
225g packaged sponge
   roll (see note)
2 quantities Vienna Cream
red food colouring
blue food colouring
purple food colouring
apricot food colouring
green food colouring
8 jube rings
thin licorice
chocolate sprinkles
coloured popcorn
1 pipecleaner
wooden iceblock sticks
20 round chocolate biscuits
assorted sweets (as shown)
1 icecream wafer
1 board, straight or curved,
   100cm x 20cm (40in x 8in)

Make cakes according to directions on packet, divide mixture evenly between four greased 25cm × 8cm (10in × 3in) bar tins, bake in moderate oven 30 minutes or until cooked when tested. Turn cakes on to wire rack to cool.

Cut bar cakes in half vertically to give eight equal pieces, reserve five of these to make tops of the four carriages and back of engine, cut remaining three pieces in half horizontally to give six equal pieces, five of which form the bases of the engine and four carriages; cut off one quarter of remaining piece to add to engine base to extend it, discard remaining three quarters. Cut a 4cm (1½in) wide slice from sponge roll, hold slice upright and cut out smoke stack shape with a 2.5cm (1in) plain cutter, as shown; use the rest of the sponge roll for engine. Assemble cake, as shown, on prepared board.

Divide Vienna Cream into five equal portions, tint one portion with red food colouring, one with blue food

colouring, one with purple food colouring, one with apricot food colouring and one with green food colouring; cover tops and sides of the engine and carriages each with different-coloured Vienna Cream, as shown. Join carriages with pairs of jube rings: split one ring, push the other ring through it, press on to Vienna Cream. Outline engine and tops of carriages with thin licorice, as shown. Cover top and sides of smoke stack with red Vienna Cream, coat with chocolate sprinkles, position, as shown; with a skewer, make holes through five pieces of popcorn, thread on to pipecleaner, insert into smoke stack.

Place whole iceblock sticks across front, back and between carriages, as shown, to represent sleepers; to make other sleepers, break iceblock sticks into 4cm (1½in) lengths, slide them underneath edges of cake on both sides. Double strips of licorice on either side of train represent tracks. Position chocolate biscuits, as shown, to represent wheels, stick round flat

sweets on chocolate biscuits with a little Vienna Cream. Cut a 4cm × 1cm (1½in × .½in) strip from wafer, press strip firmly on to bottom front of engine, arrange pieces of 2.5cm (1in) licorice against wafer, as shown, to represent "cow catcher" Pile popcorn on top of carriages, decorate rest of cake with assorted sweets.

Note: The sponge roll we used was 17cm (6½in) in length and 6cm (2½in) in diameter. Called French Sponge Roll, it was made by Top Taste.

HORSE CORRAL
1 packet butter cake mix
1 quantity Vienna Cream
1 tablespoon cocoa
green food colouring
1½ cups coconut
blue food colouring
brown food colouring
knitting wool
string
tubular licorice
small pieces ribbon
1 toy farmyard set
1 small toy cowboy

Make cake according to directions on packet, spread into greased deep 20cm (8in) round cake tin, bake in moderate oven 50 minutes, stand 3 minutes, turn on to wire rack to cool.

Place ½ cup Vienna Cream in small basin, add sifted cocoa, mix well; tint remaining Vienna Cream with a few drops green food colouring. Tint 1 cup coconut green, tint 1 tablespoon coconut blue, tint remaining coconut brown. Spread sides and 2.5cm (1in) border around top edge of cake with green-tinted Vienna Cream, sprinkle with green-tinted coconut, spread uncovered top of cake with brown-tinted Vienna Cream, sprinkle with brown-tinted coconut.

Make rope with plaited wool, make whip with plaited string, cut small pieces of ribbon for horse blankets to hang on fence. To make wagon wheel, twist one pipecleaner into circle, squeeze ends together, place half a pipecleaner across centre, wrap one end around frame of wheel, cut other end to about 3mm (⅛in) longer than frame, as shown, twist around frame; make two more spokes the same way. To make horse trough, take piece of tubular licorice 5cm (2in) long, cut open with scissors, cut small triangular pieces for ends of trough from another small piece of tubular licorice, press firmly on to ends of trough, as shown; fill trough with blue-tinted coconut to represent water. Place fence around top of cake, position cowboy with whip, decorate with plastic tree and horse, as shown.

CENTREPIECE FOR THE PARTY TABLE

Here is a gentle dragon — made of cake and sweets — that is a fun centrepiece for the party table. If you allow one packet of sweets per guest, each child can take one home.

THE DRAGON
1 packet butter cake mix
licorice allsorts
toothpicks
cardboard
aluminium foil
1 quantity Vienna Cream
apricot food colouring
23cm (9in) ribbon for tongue
assorted sweets (as shown)
cellophane paper
different-coloured ribbons

Make cake according to directions on packet, pour half mixture into greased 25cm × 8cm (10in × 3in) bar tin, pour remaining half into well-greased nut roll tin, bake in moderate oven 30 minutes for bar cake, 35 minutes for nut roll cake or until cooked when tested. Turn on to wire rack to cool.

Trim top of bar cake so it is flat, cut away sides, as shown, to make the tail. Cut nut roll cake lengthwise at a slight angle, as shown, giving a larger piece for the top and smaller piece for the base. Cut licorice allsorts into triangles of graduating size to represent teeth; insert a toothpick through two triangles of the same size, as

shown. (You will need five pairs on each side, graduating in size.)

Cut two pieces of cardboard just large enough to fit under head and tail of dragon, cover with aluminium foil. (Cardboard should not be visible; it is there simply to make dragon easier to handle.) Tint Vienna Cream with a few drops apricot food colouring, cover base piece of nut roll cake with apricot Vienna Cream; place cake on cardboard. Insert teeth into cake on both sides, as shown; position ribbon down centre for tongue. Cover top piece of nut roll cake with Vienna Cream, place carefully in position so that the toothpicks go through the cake to hold top of head firmly in place. Decorate head with assorted sweets, as shown. Cover tail with Vienna Cream, place on piece of covered cardboard, decorate with licorice allsorts triangles.

Make packets of assorted sweets with cellophane paper tied with ribbon, allowing one packet per guest; arrange packets to form body of dragon. Small jars filled with assorted sweets and decorated with ribbon could be used instead of the cellophane packets of sweets.

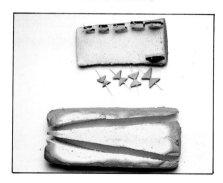

127

INDEX

Pictured opposite:
Gingerbread Man, see page 12.